DAILY LIFE IN BIBLICAL TIMES

Society of Biblical Literature

Archaeology and Biblical Studies

Andrew G. Vaughn,
Editor

Number 5

DAILY LIFE IN BIBLICAL TIMES

Daily Life in Biblical Times

by
Oded Borowski

Society of Biblical Literature
Atlanta

DAILY LIFE IN BIBLICAL TIMES

Library of Congress Cataloging-in-Publication Data

Borowski, Oded.
    Daily life in biblical times / by Oded Borowski.
        p. cm. — (Society of Biblical Literature archaeology and biblical studies ; 5)
        Includes bibliographical references and index.
    ISBN 1-58983-042-3 (pbk.)
    1. Jews—Social life and customs—To 70 A.D. 2. Palestine—Social life and customs—To 70 A.D. 3. Bible. O.T.—Antiquities. 4. Palestine—Civilization. I. Title. II. Series: Archaeology and biblical studies ; no. 5.
    DS112 .B63 2003
    221.9'5—dc21
                                             2003012930

11 10 09 08 07 06 05   5 4 3

Printed in the United States of America
on acid-free paper

CONTENTS

PREFACE ix

ABBREVIATIONS xi

1. INTRODUCTION: THE LAND AND ITS PEOPLE 1
   The Land   1
   The People   6
   The Sources   10

2. RURAL LIFE 13
   The Village   13
       Physical Layout   14
       Types of Villages   14
       The House   16
       Biblical Depictions of Village Life   21
   Sociopolitical Structure of the Village   21
       Village Government   21
       The Family   22
       Hospitality   22
       Religious Practices   24
   The Economy   25
       Agriculture   26
           Land Use   27
           The Calendar   27
           Field Crops, Fruit Trees, Vegetables, and More   28
       Herding   29
       Other Professions and Occupations   30
           Pottery Making   30
           Weaving   31
           Tanning   32
           Carpentry   33
           Masonry   33
           Metallurgy   34
   Warfare: The Early Years   35
       Ideology   36

         Strategy and Tactics   37
         Results of War   41

3. URBAN LIFE 43
    The City   43
         City Planning   44
              City Types   44
              Fortifications   46
              Water Systems   49
              Palaces and Other Accommodations   49
         Population   52
         Religion   54
    The Economy   55
         Trade and Commerce   55
              Overland Trade   56
              Maritime Commerce   58
    When the Kings Went to War   59

4. THE HOUSEHOLD AND LIFE CYCLES 63
    The Israelite Diet   63
         Food Resources   63
         The Menu   65
              Baked Goods   65
              Dairy Products   66
              Meat Dishes   67
              Seafood   68
              Fowl   69
              Fruit and Fruit Products   70
              Drinks   70
              Other Foods   71
              Spices and Condiments   72
         Food Storage   72
         Food Preparation and Consumption   73
    Health and Sickness   74
    Hygiene and Sanitation   78
         Personal Hygiene   78
         Sanitation   79
    Life Cycles   80
         Birth   81
         Marriage   81
         Death and Burial   83

5. ANCIENT ISRAELITE ARTS 87
    Performing Arts: Music and Dance   87
        Biblical Music and Musical Instruments   88
        Musical Notes   90
    Musical Performance   90
        Private Performance   90
        Public Performance   91
            Secular Occurrences   91
            Religious Occurrences   92
    Visual Arts   93
        Ivory   93
        Clay   94
        Glyptic Art   96
        Mixed Media   97

6. WRITING—PRIVATE AND OFFICIAL 99
    Private   100
    Official Writings   101
        Correspondence   102
        Record Keeping   103
        Chronicles   104
        Monumental Inscriptions   105
    Miscellaneous Inscriptions   106
    Creative Writing   106

7. A DAY IN THE LIFE OF THE AHUZAM FAMILY 109

NOTES 127

INDEX OF BIBLICAL REFERENCES 139
INDEX OF MODERN AUTHORITIES 145
INDEX OF HEBREW WORDS..147

PREFACE

For everything there is a season,	and for every activity under heaven its time:
a time to be born	and a time to die;
a time to plant	and a time to uproot;
a time to kill	and a time to heal;
a time to break down	and a time to build up;
a time to weep	and a time to laugh;
a time to mourn	and a time to dance;
a time to cast stones	and a time to gather them;
a time to embrace	and a time to refrain from embracing;
a time to seek	and a time to lose;
a time to keep	and a time to discard;
a time to tear	and a time to mend;
a time to be silent	and a time to speak up;
a time to love	and a time to hate;
a time for war	and a time for peace.

Ecclesiastes 3:1–8

The Israelite period, starting with the Israelite tribal confederacy (ca. 1200 B.C.E.) through the time of the monarchy to the fall of the Solomonic temple (587/586 B.C.E.), was a relatively long period. While the history of this period has been in the forefront of biblical research, little attention has been paid to the context in which historical events took place.[1] Where did the Israelites live? What did people do for a living? How did the family function? What did they eat, and what affected their health? These and similar questions form the basis for this book. The book aims to introduce the different aspects of daily life during the Israelite period. These aspects include the lay of the land and the people who occupied it. It deals with the economy, whether rural or urban, with special emphasis on the main sources of livelihood, such as agriculture, herding, and trade. Since not everyone was engaged in these occupations, other professions and means of livelihood are described. Another important topic is the social structure in general and the family in particular. Beyond material culture, the book delves into daily and seasonal cultural, social and religious activities and different art modes, such as music, and the place of writing in Israelite society. The book uses primary evidence such as the Bible, extrabiblical records from ancient Palestine and neighboring societies, and archaeology. Secondary sources are also consulted.

The book is aimed at undergraduate and graduate students, teachers, and other interested readers not specializing in the topic but curious about it. Scholars dealing with textual analysis who need to understand the background for the texts they study can use this book. The book provides context for the text. It is written in a readable language, contains several illustrations and indexes, and a bibliography for further reading. The aim of this work is not to cover every historical-cultural aspect of the ancient Near East. I assume that the reader either has some prior knowledge or will seek more information with the aid of the bibliographies cited here.

This book integrates and continues my previous work on agriculture and the daily use of animals in biblical times.[2] As in my previous works, I refer to the area on the eastern shore of the Mediterranean Sea during the period before the appearance of the Israelites as Canaan; this area is referred to as Eretz Yisrael during the time of the Israelite presence. As a geographical reference to the region, I employ the terms Palestine and Syria-Palestine, both of which are broad and should not be construed in the present-day political sense. The period covered in this book is between roughly 1200–586 B.C.E., known in the scholarly literature as the Iron Age and the Israelite period. The early Iron Age (ca. 1200–1000 B.C.E.) is known as Iron Age I and the settlement period, while the later portion of the period is divided into the united monarchy (ca. 1000–920 B.C.E.) and the divided monarchy (ca. 920–586 B.C.E.). The monarchical period is also known as Iron Age II, and some scholars refer to the period between the fall of Samaria (722 B.C.E.) and the fall of Jerusalem (586 B.C.E.) as Iron Age III.

Like many other books, the writing of this book benefited from the help extended by many. First, I would like to thank Andrew G. Vaughn, the series editor, for asking me to write this book and for his constructive comments throughout the process. Furthermore, I would like to thank the anonymous proposal readers who, during its inception, helped shape the book with their timely constructive suggestions. A very important source of inspiration has been several generations of my students who participated in my course on Daily Life in Ancient Israel. I owe a debt of gratitude to Bob Buller for the beautiful layout of the book and for his work on the indices. Finally, I would like to thank my wife Marcia for enabling me to immerse myself in this project. Additionally, I would like to acknowledge Emory University for providing me with a sabbatical leave during which the book was written. I hope this book will provide the pertinent information to those seeking it.

ABBREVIATIONS

ABD	*Anchor Bible Dictionary*. Edited by D. N. Freedman. 6 vols. New York: Doubleday, 1992.
ANET	*Ancient Near Eastern Texts Relating to the Old Testament*. Edited by J. B. Pritchard. 3d ed. Princeton, N.J.: Princeton University Press, 1969.
BA	*Biblical Archaeologist*
BAR	*Biblical Archaeology Review*
BASOR	*Bulletin of the American Schools of Oriental Research*
CANE	*Civilizations of the Ancient Near East*. Edited by J. Sasson. 4 vols. New York: Scribner, 1995.
ErIsr	*Eretz-Israel*
EDB	*Eerdman's Dictionary of the Bible*. Edited by D. N. Freedman. Grand Rapids: Eerdmans, 2000.
HBD	*HarperCollins Bible Dictionary*. Edited by P. J. Achtemeier et al. 2d ed. San Francisco: HarperCollins, 1996.
HSM	Harvard Semitic Monographs
IEJ	*Israel Exploration Journal*
JSOTSup	Journal for the Study of the Old Testament Supplement Series
OLA	Orientalia lovaniensia analecta
SBLABS	Society of Biblical Literature Archaeology and Biblical Studies

1
INTRODUCTION: THE LAND AND ITS PEOPLE

When coming to discuss the daily life of any people, it is important to identify and define the factors and conditions that caused and influenced the formation, and later sustained, the culture of that group. This includes a thorough examination of the region in which these people lived and the environment in which they operated. The people who are the subject of the study need to be described in as precise terms as possible, including their origins and numbers. The sources for these determinations and for the whole study need to be articulated so the conclusions can be examined time and again.

THE LAND

Many cultures, ancient and recent, owe their particular character to the environment in which they have developed. Geography, topography, climate, and other ecological factors mold each culture and help in the formation of its unique character. Ancient Israel was no different, and to be able to understand Israel it is necessary to understand its background, including the natural conditions that gave birth to this entity. Amihai Mazar's words explain it well:

> The geographic location of the country determined its important role in the history of the ancient Near East. On the one hand, this region formed a bridge between the two ends of the Fertile Crescent: Egypt on the south and Syria and Mesopotamia in the north; on the other hand, it was compressed between the Mediterranean Sea on the west and the desert to the east. This unique situation was the basic factor in the country's history and cultural development. More than any other country in the ancient world, this land was always directly or indirectly connected with other parts of the Near East and the eastern Mediterranean.[1]

Eretz Yisrael[2] is situated in the eastern Mediterranean Basin, generally in the same latitude as southern Spain, the state of Georgia (United States), and Baja California (Mexico). While this area developed its own civilization, its location between the two great valley civilizations of the Nile and

Mesopotamia, from whence came armies as well as merchants, contributed to many of its cultural elements. The inhabitants of this land bridge were greatly influenced not only by the Egyptians, and Assyrians, but also by the Hittites, Hurrians, Babylonians, Persians, and later on by the Greeks and Romans (see fig. 1.1).

The land that was settled by the Israelites, from the eastern coast of the Mediterranean (the Great Sea) in the west to the desert in the east, and from Mount Hermon (in modern Lebanon) in the north to the Gulf of Eilat (or Aqaba) in the south,[3] is composed of several ecological zones distinguished from each other by differences in topography and climate, both of which have affected the flora and fauna. These, in turn, had great influence on the way of life in general and the dominating economy in particular, which further contributed to the evolution of other cultural aspects, such as religion as well as the social and political structures.

Some of these zones are mentioned and described in the Bible, especially in the book of Joshua, which is replete with geographical information. The descriptions of the wars and conquests and the allotment of territories to the tribes contain references to geographical regions such as "the hill country, the Negev, the Shephelah, [and] the watersheds" (Josh 10:40). Because of the geological history of the entire area, most of these regions are in a north-south orientation and align along the spine of the hill country (*har;* Josh 11:2; 12:8), which is also subdivided into several blocks. The most northern, the Galilee, is divided into Upper and Lower Galilee, with its northernmost edge reaching Mount Hermon (Josh 12:1; 13:5), the southernmost edge of the Lebanon Mountains. The Galilee is a rugged area, not easy to be settled, with mountains as high as 3,962 feet. Further south is another block known as Mount Ephraim (*har 'eprāyim,* Josh 17:15) or the hill country of Israel (*har yiśrā'ēl,* Josh 11:16, 21), reaching a height of 3,083–3,332 feet, with several intermountain valleys fit for agriculture. Connected to this block is another known as the hill country of Judah (*har yəhûdâ,* Josh 11:21), with heights of 1,948–3,310 feet. The latter is not as hospitable for agricultural pursuit as Mount Ephraim.

Between the northern mountain block (Galilee) and Mount Ephraim, in an east-west orientation, stretches the large Jezreel Valley, the breadbasket of Palestine, and to its east a smaller valley known as Beth-shean Valley.

West of the highlands and along the coast runs the coastal plain, the central part of which is named Sharon in the Bible (Isa 33:9). At its north, the Sharon is interrupted by Mount Carmel (Josh 19:26), which slopes steeply into the Mediterranean. During the beginning of Iron Age I, the southern continuation of the coastal plain was settled by a group of the Sea Peoples known in the Bible as Philistines, while parts of the northern stretch of the coastal plain around Dor were settled by two other Sea Peoples groups, the Sikils and Shardanu, and by the coastal Canaanites, the

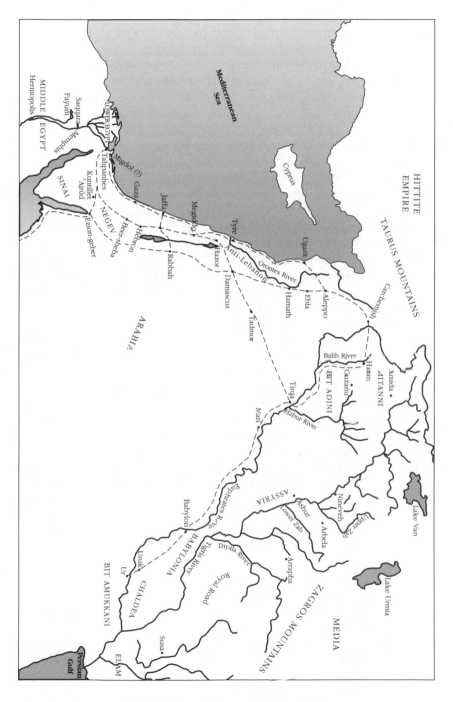

Fig. 1.1. Map of the ancient Near East.

Phoenicians. The latter occupied mainly the coastal area from the Carmel northward into the region of present-day Lebanon.[4] A zone of low hills, known in the Bible as the Shephelah (Josh 9:1), runs between the southern coastal plain and the highlands of Judah. This area, which is an ecological meeting place between the coastal plain, the hill country, and the desert, was also a cultural and political meeting place between the Israelites and Philistines. South of the highlands of Judah lies the Beersheba Valley and the Negev Desert, stretching all the way to the Gulf of Eilat (Aqaba).

Immediately east of the highlands a deep valley runs from north to south, with the Jordan River meandering through from the foot of Mount Hermon to the Salt Sea or Sea of the Araba, known today as the Dead Sea, the lowest point on earth (1,285 ft. below sea level). The zone between the highlands and the Jordan River, from the Beth-shean Valley to the Salt Sea, is arid, rugged, and desertlike. It was always a place favored by runaways and hermits. East of the Jordan River, in Transjordan, rises a high plateau (as high as 4,090 ft.), the northern part of which is covered with basalt emitted by now-extinct volcanoes.

In antiquity as in modern times, the main and secondary roads followed the topography. The major arteries generally followed a north-south orientation along the seacoast, the mountain chains, and the valleys, connecting the main centers of civilization, Egypt and Mesopotamia. The secondary, or local, roads connected the main cities with their dependencies, the small towns, villages, and farmsteads. They crisscrossed the countryside, also following the terrain (see fig. 1.2).[5]

Two bodies of water, actually small lakes, are strung along the Jordan: one (now drained) is known as Lake Huleh; south of it is the Sea of Kinnereth, or Sea of Galilee. Between the Salt Sea and the Gulf of Eilat runs a broad, level valley known as the Araba. The long valley from the Hermon Mountain down to the Gulf of Eilat is part of a geological phenomenon, the Syrian-African Rift.

Water is the most important element for sustaining life. Without water, no human, animal, or plant can survive. Unfortunately, water sources are scarce in this region, and dependency on rain (and dew) is quite high. The availability of water is limited to several brooks running west from the highlands into the Mediterranean or east into the Jordan River or the lakes. Other brooks run west into the Jordan Valley from the Transjordanian Plateau. Most of the brooks in the region between the Judean Mountains and the Syrian-African Rift are dry riverbeds (wadis) that get filled only when rain falls on the eastern slopes of this mountain range.

Other natural water sources include a limited number of perennial springs around which settlements were established and maintained

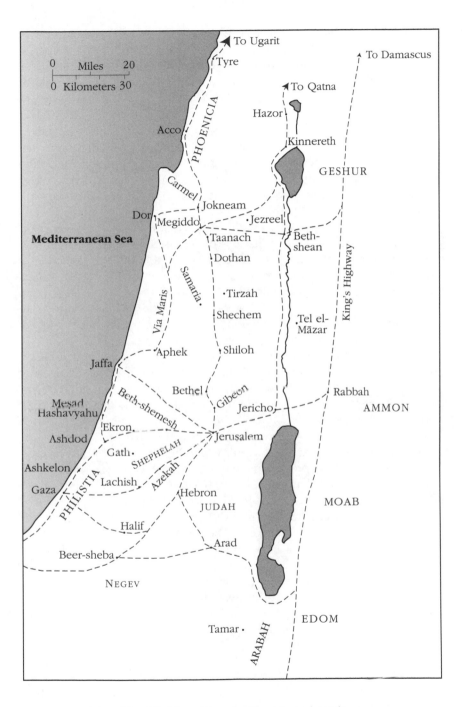

Fig. 1.2. Map of Israel with sites and roads.

throughout history. Some of these springs help support oases, especially in the Negev and the Araba. In certain places along the Jordan Valley there are hot springs oozing mineral waters; these are remnants and indicators of the tectonic activity prevalent in the Near East, where earthquakes were partially responsible for shaping the landscape and have been known to occur throughout history.

The response of humankind to the scarcity of natural water sources has been varied. It includes digging wells to reach ground water, constructing cisterns and pools to collect runoff water, building channels and diversion dams, hewing shafts and tunnels to reach and divert water sources, and developing different ways to efficiently store, conserve, and use water.

While the country is agriculturally rich (Deut 8:8), it is mineral poor. The latter is in spite of the fact that the Bible describes it as rich with iron and copper (Deut 8:9). However, limestone available all over the country and basalt stone in the north were used in the construction of buildings and in the manufacture of certain tools and installations. While large parts of the country were forested, local wood was used in private construction; cedars were imported from Lebanon for many of the public buildings (1 Kgs 5:22, 24 [Eng. 5:8, 10]).

The climate in this region has two major seasons, winter and summer, and two transitional, autumn and spring. This division is depicted in many mosaic floors from the late Roman-Byzantine period. The autumn and winter are the rainy seasons. In a normal year the rain begins in October (*yôreh*),[6] with most of it falling during the winter, December through March. At times conditions are ripe for snow and hail. Some late rains (*malqôš*) fall in the early spring, April, while the summer, June to August, is almost dry, with dews providing the only moisture. Precipitation is higher in the north (40–60 in.) than in the south (0–10 in.) and in the west than in the east. The least precipitation is on the eastern slopes of the Ephraim and Judean highlands (10–20 in.) and in the Negev and the Araba (0–10 in.).

Temperatures and humidity vary. The mean temperature in Jerusalem in January is about 47°F, but in August 75°F. On the coast (in modern Tel Aviv) the mean temperature in January is 55°F and in August 81°F. Generally, the most warm and most dry region is around the Dead Sea and along the Araba to the Gulf of Eilat. The Beth-shean Valley is also very hot but also humid. Summertime is also when the east wind (in Arabic, *ḥamsîn*) blows in from the desert (*rûaḥ haqqādîm*, Ezek 17:10).

THE PEOPLE

Who were the people we refer to as Israelites? Recently, many scholars have attempted to identify these people, their ancestry and their place of origin.[7] Were they outsiders who arrived in the land and conquered it as described in the Bible, or did they get there in some other way? Were they descendants of the local population, known in the Bible as Canaanites, who for whatever reason formed a new entity, known to us as Israel? Were the formation processes simple enough for us to be able to reconstruct them from the available information, or were they so complicated that we will never be able to find the complete answer?

The Bible maintains that when the Israelites appeared on the scene, the land was already occupied by certain groups, the names of which include not only the Canaanites but also "the Amorites, Hittites, Perizzites, and Jebusites in the hill country, and the Hivites below Hermon in the land of Mizpah" (Josh 11:3).[8] There were also others, including the Philistines. For the purpose of the present discussion, I accept the proposal that an Israelite entity, possibly referred to in the Merneptah Stela as Israel,[9] was developed in the hill country of Israel and Judah during the Iron Age I (twelfth-eleventh century B.C.E.) and that their origin was varied.[10] I also accept the notion that certain aspects characteristic of Iron Age I settlements such as pottery and architecture reflect environmental, social, and economic traits of the settlers rather than their ethnicity. Furthermore, I accept the notion that "the rise of early Israel was the latest phase in *long-term, cyclic processes* of settlement oscillation and rise and fall of territorial entities in the highlands" of Cis- and Transjordan that started earlier in the Early and Middle Bronze Ages.[11]

It is almost impossible to know what the Iron Age I settlers looked like, because of a dearth in artistic representations illustrating their physical attributes and clothing. Frank J. Yurco, however attributes the Karnak reliefs to Merneptah and suggests that in part they portray the Israel-people of the Merneptah Stela.[12] Their physical appearance is no different from that of the Canaanites depicted in the other parts of the reliefs. The physical appearance of the Iron Age II Israelites can be gleaned mainly from two Assyrian monuments. One is the Black Obelisk of Shalmaneser III (ca. 858–824 B.C.E.), which shows Jehu king of Israel wearing an ankle-long tunic and a hat and prostrating before the Assyrian king (fig. 1.3).[13] The other is Sennacherib's reliefs, which celebrate the capture of Lachish (701 B.C.E.). The latter reliefs depict the Judahite defenders fighting off the Assyrians from on top of the city walls and its towers. A closer look at individual citizens of Lachish is available in scenes showing whole families leaving the city (see fig. 1.4).[14] The females wear long dresses and a long head-cover reaching their ankles. The males wear a tunic reaching just above their knees, held in place with a wide belt and a wrap-around headdress. Males not wearing a headdress exhibit curly hair. Males also have a beard. Both males and females are barefoot, but biblical references indicate that people wore sandals. Other hints concerning the appearance of the Israelites can be gleaned from skeletal remains and verbal descriptions (see below under The Sources).

What was the language used by the Israelites? The written sources left by the Israelites indicate that their language belonged to the West-Semitic family, akin to Canaanite, Moabite, Ammonite, and other languages spoken by the different inhabitants of the region. Written sources such as the Bible and the Gezer Calendar show that the northern Israelites spoke with a dialect different from the one spoken in Jerusalem. The latter is referred to in 2 Kgs 18:26 and Isa 36:11 as Judahite (yəhûdît). In the same biblical verses it is pointed out that members of the upper class were familiar with Aramaic: "Then Eliakim, Shebna, and Joah said to the Rabshakeh, 'Please speak to your servants in Aramaic, for we understand it; do not speak to us in Judahite within the hearing of the people who are on the wall'" (For more on the language, see ch. 6.)

Fig. 1.3. Black Obelisk of Shalmaneser III. Courtesy British Museum.

Several recent studies have attempted to estimate the size of this population as well as the population during the monarchical period.[15] Estimates of the highlands population during Iron Age I place it at about 20,000 in 1200 B.C.E. and about 55,000 in 1000 B.C.E.;[16] estimation of the united kingdom's population in Cis- and Transjordan suggests 350,000.[17] The population in Cisjordan at the height of the Iron Age II (eighth century B.C.E.) has been recently estimated at 400,000,[18] while in Transjordan the Israelite population is estimated at 60,000 and the non-Israelite population at 43,500. For the same period, the population of Philistia has been estimated at 50,000. However, Assyrian campaigns and especially Sennacherib's campaign in 701 B.C.E. caused a sharp decline, and the population of Judah for that period is estimated at about 100,000 at a much higher density.[19] Most of the Iron Age II population (66 percent) resided in small villages and the rest in settlements (towns, cities) larger than twelve acres. The rise in number of small villages during the Iron Age II is attributed to the relative stability and tranquillity offered by the monarchies.[20]

Fig. 1.4. Lachish Reliefs, Israelite captives. Courtesy David Ussishkin.

Demographic studies show that during the Iron Age, once a foothold was established in the highlands, the evolving political conditions helped improve the socioeconomic conditions, which in turn led to a population increase that was manifested in the establishment of new, and the enlargement and strengthening of old, settlements throughout the country.

THE SOURCES

To reconstruct daily life during any historical period, one needs to identify the proper sources. For the present study, the Hebrew Bible is a primary source of information. Despite the ongoing argument concerning its date of composition and reliability, the Hebrew Bible contains very useful information for the reconstruction of daily life. Besides the Hebrew Bible, other sources were consulted. These include extrabiblical written records from Palestine and the surrounding cultures, including Canaanite, Egyptian, and Mesopotamian. To illustrate many of the topics described in the written records, I have considered and included when possible artistic representations from the various cultures of the ancient Near East as well as other archaeological evidence, such as tools and installations. Unfortunately, little skeletal evidence is available for the reconstruction of the physical appearance of the Israelites, but I hope that with all the other multiple resources I can present a rounded and comprehensive picture of daily life in Iron Age Israel.

FOR FURTHER STUDY

Aharoni, Yohanan, and Michael Avi-Yonah. *The Macmillan Bible Atlas.* New York: Macmillan, 1968.
> An excellent atlas written by two eminent scholars, one specializing in the earlier periods and the other in the later periods of Israelite and Jewish history. The atlas presents visual background to many events mentioned in the Bible and in extrabiblical sources and provides maps of the Near East and Palestine from the earliest historical periods to the rise of the church.

Dever, William G. *What Did the Biblical Writers Know and When Did They Know It?* Grand Rapids: Eerdmans, 2001.
> A good summary of the ongoing debate between the "minimalists" and "maximalists" concerning the origins of the biblical text and its reliability for writing Israelite history. Furthermore, the book contains chapters presenting archaeological remains and their relationship to biblical history and to daily life in the biblical period.

Finkelstein, Israel. *The Archaeology of the Israelite Settlement.* Translated by D. Saltz. Jerusalem: Israel Exploration Society, 1988.

The question of the Israelite settlement in Canaan must be resolved on the basis of archaeological evidence. This book, which is based on extensive surveys of the hill country, is an excellent source of data concerning the appearance of the so-called "Proto-Israelites" and the mark they left on the land.

Hallo, William W., and K. Lawson Younger Jr., eds. *The Context of Scripture*. 3 vols. Leiden: Brill, 1997–.

The most up-to-date source for ancient Near Eastern texts related to the Hebrew Bible (abbr. *COS*).

Mazar, Amihai. *Archaeology of the Land of the Bible: 10,000–586 B.C.E.* New York: Doubleday, 1990.

A highly detailed book by a leading Israeli archaeologist on the archaeology of Palestine from the prehistoric periods to the fall of the First Temple. This is a good introduction to each of the periods and issues dealt with by biblical archaeologists and could be used as a textbook for advanced students.

Pritchard, James B., ed. *Ancient Near Eastern Texts Relating to the Old Testament*. 3d ed. Princeton, N.J.: Princeton University Press, 1969.

A very good resource for extrabiblical documents illuminating the biblical world. It presents literary, legal, and other types of documents from Egypt, Mesopotamia, Anatolia, and Palestine that relate to biblical events and provides the necessary background for understanding the world of the Bible (abbr. *ANET*).

2

RURAL LIFE

The Village

While some of the older Late Bronze Age cities in the lowlands still survived in the Iron Age I (ca. 1200–1000 B.C.E.), either as a simple continuation of the earlier city-states or as newly expanded Philistine urban centers, new and mostly rural settlements developed in the hill country in various layouts, representing a variety of subsistence economies. A unique opportunity to see the complex and gradual processes of social change is presented by the relatively large number of excavated Iron Age IA sites.

> The rural settlements of the hill-country and the Beersheba valley provide assorted examples of site plans that represent communities on the continuum between semi-nomadic pastoralists and fully settled farmers. These sites include encampments with storage pits for rich crop yields obtained by pastoral nomads, like Stratum IX at Tel Beersheba, clusters of animals pens like Giloh, enclosed settlements like Beersheba Stratum VII, or large groups of such units as at Stratum II at Tel Masos. Finally, full-scale villages were exposed at sites like 'Ai and Stratum III at Beth Shemesh.[1]

The popularity of village life was not limited to Iron Age I. In the Iron Age II (ca. 1000–sixth century B.C.E.) most of the population (66 percent) resided in small villages and the rest in settlements (towns, cities) larger than twelve acres. The growth of the village trend, or process, that started at end of the Late Bronze Age–beginning of Iron Age I is attributed to the relative stability and tranquility provided by the Israelite monarchies.[2] Others think that the expanding number of villages in the Iron Age II was the outcome of the changing character of the cities during this urban phase. They were gradually filled up by nonresidential structures, which forced most of their inhabitants to leave. The cities became occupied predominantly by members of the state administration. Thus, the bulk of the population moved out of the cities into the countryside to live in villages and farmsteads.[3]

Since the village was the main living locus during the Israelite period, we begin our exploration with an examination of life in the village.

13

PHYSICAL LAYOUT

Surveys and excavations show that villages were located on non-agricultural lands. Agricultural land, no matter where but especially in the hill country, was extremely precious, since it was the outcome of a concerted effort of land clearing of trees and stones and of terrace building.[4] Unlike present-day practices, no farmer would have sacrificed agricultural land, which was the product of hard work, for a nonproductive purpose such as house construction.[5] Therefore, villages were built on rocky outcrops or steep slopes and possibly on a hilltop for some measure of defense. However, they were established close enough to the fields, no more than walking distance. Most villages were established in previously unsettled locations, although some were on the ruins of long-abandoned sites.[6] Furthermore, most villages were situated near country roads that provided communication with other villages and with the "mother" city. The relationship between a city and its surrounding villages is portrayed in the Bible as that of mother and daughters, as is repeatedly mentioned in some of the tribal lists of land allocation: "In Issachar and Asher, Manasseh possessed Beth-shean and her daughters [bənôtêhā],[7] Ibleam and her daughters, the inhabitants of Dor and her daughters, the inhabitants of Endor and her daughters, the inhabitants of Taanach and her daughters, and the inhabitants of Megiddo and her daughters" (Josh 17:11). This warm relationship must have been the result of political, military (defense), and economic bonds.

Several characteristics distinguish the Iron Age villages from other settlements such as towns and cities. No village has yet yielded either monumental buildings or cult centers that can be interpreted as public.[8] The cult places must have been located outside the villages in the open countryside.[9] Villages were unfortified, "although occasionally the houses situated on the edge of the settlement [were] set out in a manner of a defensive ring."[10] The interior of such villages does not exhibit any trace of major preplanning. Streets and houses were positioned irregularly, and at times open areas and numerous grain pits were incorporated inside the villages.

Villages were located in close proximity to natural, perennial water sources such as springs, streams, and brooks. Where natural water sources were lacking, wells were dug to reach the ground-water level; cisterns to collect rainwater were also hewn in bedrock inside the village.

TYPES OF VILLAGES

Based on archaeological evidence, we can distinguish three forms of settlement: ring-shaped villages; agglomerated villages; and farmsteads.[11]

1. In ring-shaped villages, the houses are in a closed circle or oval, with an open space in the middle that could have been used for sheltering

domestic animals. Some scholars say that these must have been the biblical *ḥǎṣērîm* mentioned frequently in the book of Joshua (e.g., 15:32).[12] In
ʿIzbet Ṣarṭah (in central Israel) Stratum III, the ring is made out of broadroom houses built next to each other (see fig. 2.1), while in Beer-sheba
Stratum VII the houses are mostly of the four-room type.[13]

2. Agglomerated villages are characterized by "indiscriminate construction that has taken place on the site, in the form of individual buildings or
complexes consisting of several houses."[14] Living space is restricted,
streets vary in width, and irregular open areas were left between dwelling
units. Since the houses were situated without plan, the edge of the village
was left open. Villages of this type were uncovered at ʿAi, Khirbet Rad-
dana (north of Jerusalem), ʿIzbet Ṣarṭah Stratum II, Ḥorvat Masos (Kh.
el-Meshash; near Beer-sheba) Stratum II (see fig. 2.2), and Beer-sheba
Stratum VI.[15]

3. Farmsteads are made of a single building or a group of buildings
surrounded by a widely extending wall, not for defensive purposes but to
form an enclosure for domestic animals. One example for such a settlement is Giloh, near Jerusalem (see fig. 2.3).[16]

The physical setting of the village, with its open public spaces especially by the gate, offered a locus for carrying out public business such as

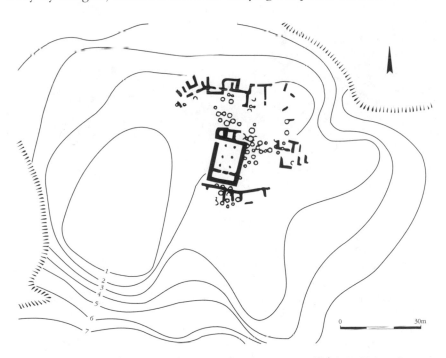

Fig. 2.1. Plan of ʿIzbet Ṣarṭah. Courtesy Ze'ev Herzog, Tel Aviv University.

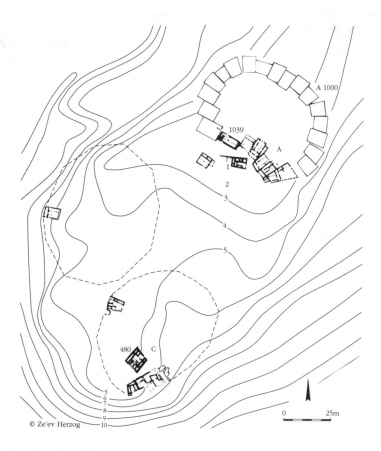

Fig. 2.2. Plan of Ḥorvat Masos. Courtesy Ze'ev Herzog, Tel Aviv University.

commerce and judicial proceedings (e.g., Deut 21:18–19; 22:15, 24; Amos 5:12, 15; Ruth 4:1–11).

THE HOUSE

The family, which was the focal point of village life, resided in the house, known in the Bible as "father's house" (*bêt 'āb*).[17] There was more than one house type or one house configuration. The broadroom houses of ʿIzbet Ṣarṭah Stratum III were an early and an uncommon form of a dwelling house in the Iron Age I, when many of the villages in the highlands were established. It is still debatable how much room space of this house type was roofed over, so it is hard to ascertain where certain activities took place inside the house. Most scholars identify the four-room house and its variants as the prevalent house of the Iron Age I and II.[18]

The term *four-room house* is applied to a building that is not only divided lengthwise by two rows of stone pillars but also has an additional long room in the back. According to some scholars, the four-room house

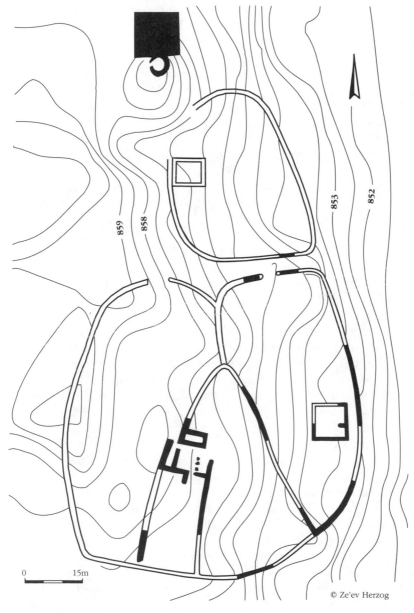

© Ze'ev Herzog

Fig. 2.3. Plan of Giloh. Courtesy Ze'ev Herzog, Tel Aviv University.

was centered upon the back room.[19] This new house type appeared at the end of the Late Bronze Age–beginning of the Early Iron Age in Cis- and Transjordan and in parts of present-day Syria and Lebanon.[20] Within a short period, it replaced the traditional courtyard house that was common in the Middle and Late Bronze Ages, although sometimes both types existed side by side.[21] The term *four-room house* was given on the basis of the floor plan, which relied mostly on remains of wall foundations. Some scholars consider the term to be misleading, because they suggest that the central part was a courtyard, with the entrance normally leading into it. They consider it a particular form of the courtyard house but suggest that the common nomenclature should be retained in order to avoid misunderstandings.[22] The *four-room house* designation is even more misleading because it appears that these houses had a second story with additional rooms upstairs. Related to this is the question whether the second story covered the whole building or only part of the ground floor. While Ehud Netzer presents both options, it would appear to be more logical and more efficient to cover the whole of the ground floor whenever possible. Thus, the central part of the second story was probably left uncovered and served as an open space.[23] A study analyzing assemblages found in different rooms concludes that at Beer-sheba the central space of the ground floor was roofed over and was used for storage and seasonal activities such as weaving. This is followed by the suggestion that the open flat roof was used for activities such as drying commodities, and sleeping (see fig. 2.4).[24]

That the four-room house had a second story is indicated by the discovery of stone steps leading upstairs and by the distinctive strong stone pillars that must have supported a heavy load such as a second or maybe even a third story.[25] Furthermore, at certain sites, such as Tell Halif in the southern Shephelah, clear architectural and stratigraphical evidence such as grindstones and clay vessels on top of second-story remains indicates the existence of that feature. The combined height of both stories was probably no more than 4–5 meters, with a low first floor.[26]

Biblical references indicate the existence of a second story. One example is related to Elijah's sojourn in Zarephath, where a "roof chamber" ('ăliyyâ) is mentioned (1 Kgs 17:19, 23). That roof chambers were living spaces is illustrated by the fact that a well-to-do Shunammite woman offered to construct for Elisha "a small roof chamber and put in it a bed, a table, a seat, and a lamp" (2 Kgs 4:10). It seems that "small" for the Shunammite woman was a relative term, since its size enabled her to furnish the room quite adequately.[27] Since the roof was flat, it was used in the winter to collect rainwater that was diverted with the help of spouts to collection areas such as cisterns. That when possible the roof was a place used for living and other activities is also apparent from the Deuteronomic

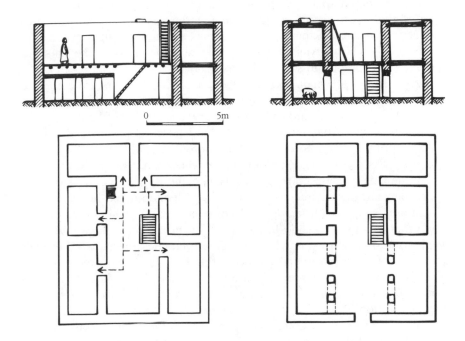

Fig. 2.4. Plan and cutout of a four-room house. Courtesy Israel Exploration Society.

law that states: "When you build a new house, put a parapet along the roof, or you will bring the guilt of bloodshed on your house if anyone should fall from it" (Deut 22:8). The use of the roof for sleeping is illustrated when at Samuel's behest "a bed was spread on the roof for Saul, and he stayed there that night" (1 Sam 9:25).[28]

The entrance to the house was into the central space of the ground floor, which served as communication area. The rest of the ground floor was used for various domestic activities such as storage of commodities and food preparation. Certain paved and unpaved areas in the side rooms were most likely used for keeping animals such as sheep, goats, and a donkey or two.[29] At some sites, cooking facilities have been uncovered in closed rooms of the ground floor, but most were near doors leading outside.[30] Light and air reached the ground floor through the main doorway, through an opening in the ceiling that allowed access by ladder to the second story, and probably also through the gaps deliberately left between the beams (or branches) that were used in the construction of the floor of the upper level. No archaeological information is available concerning the structure and shape of windows. Light was also provided by using oil lamps. The central space of the upper story was left unroofed; thus the floor of the second story could serve not only as communication area between the rooms on that story but also as a conduit of light and air for the ground floor. This was afforded by leaving gaps between the slats that made the floor. Although some scholars maintain that the back room of the ground floor was the main room, or living quarters,[31] others are correct in suggesting that "the main living area must have been on the second floor, around the upper courtyard, which was airy, had plenty of light, and was isolated from the inhabitants of the ground floor—the chickens, sheep, goats and cattle quartered there."[32] The unroofed central area of the second story was a place where domestic activities could be performed and where the family group could gather. Hence, the upper level replaced the open courtyard that characterized the earlier Mediterranean house type.[33]

Houses were constructed mostly of sun-dried mud bricks placed on stone foundations set inside foundation trenches. The ceilings and roofs were made of crossbeams with a cover of branches or reeds. The walls and the roof were plastered, a process that had to be repeated every so often because of the erosion effect caused by the rain. It should be noted that no four-room house in a village setting yielded any hint of sanitary accommodations.

Biblical information concerning furniture in the village house is limited. The inventory included "a bed, a table, a seat, and a lamp" (2 Kgs 4:10). In this respect, archaeology is not helpful at all because furniture made of perishable materials such as wood cannot be recovered. Artistic representations cannot help either because they depict objects belonging to the rich. Therefore, we need to use our imagination and ethnological comparisons made of societies still living in similar conditions, including farming villages, bedouin tents, and cave dwellings. Generally speaking, most of the items used in the homes in these cultures are made of soft materials and include skins and furs, blankets, pillows, and other items spread on the floor. For work, benches and shelves made of stones and mortar are prevalent. Niches and benches built in and around the walls are used for storage and seating. Storage of liquids is done in large vessels; grain is stored in sun-dried mud-and-straw containers. Such items must have been utilized also by the Israelites, and because of the perishable nature of most of them they did not survive. A household's richness and status can be judged by the vessels it uses for serving food. A rich household tends to entertain more, so it is expected that this will be reflected in the number of serving vessels. In Beer-sheba, House 855 is an example of a house of a well-to-do family.[34]

For the expanding *bêt 'āb,* it is suggested that whenever possible, as in Khirbet Jamain, new four-room houses were built adjacent to the old ones.[35] Under dense urban conditions this house type became common especially when buildings were close to each other with no possibility of enlarging horizontally. The two stories made it possible to use the houses more efficiently as far as storage, keeping animals, and housing a large number of humans.[36]

BIBLICAL DEPICTIONS OF VILLAGE LIFE

Glimpses of village life are afforded by the stories of the concubine in Gibeah of Benjamin (Judg 19:16–27) and Boaz and Ruth (Ruth 4). In settlements with no inns, local people were expected to invite out-of-towners into their homes. To be invited, out-of-towners would sit in the street or town square (*raḥôb*) and wait for an invitation by one of the locals (Judg 19:15). This was done probably by the entrance to the village, where people used to pass (Ruth 4:1). The houses were large enough to accommodate the guests and their animals (Judg 19:21) and were secured against intruders by strong doors (19:22, 27). Houses were so close to each other that the neighbors could tell when guests were visiting (19:22). Further, the village population was small enough that the arrival of an outsider was noticed and quickly broadcast (Ruth 2:11).

SOCIOPOLITICAL STRUCTURE OF THE VILLAGE

Although village society, at least in the beginning, was economically egalitarian, there was a certain hierarchy in social and political matters. The primary responsibility for maintaining law and order was placed on both parents (Deut 21:18; 22:15).[37] Next in line was the extended family (*bêt ʾāb*), which belonged to a larger unit, the clan (*mišpāḥâ*), which in turn was the basis for the village society.[38] Because the village was the primary socioeconomic unit, its governing system was in charge of keeping the peace.

VILLAGE GOVERNMENT

If matters got out of hand and could not be resolved inside the family, the village elders were in charge of maintaining law and order and carrying out justice. The book of Deuteronomy describes it clearly: "then his father and mother are to lay hold of him and bring him out to the elders of the town" [*ziqnê hāʿîr*]" (Deut 21:19). The elders represented the village not only in intra- but also in intervillage matters (Deut 21:1–9). They assembled for judgment "at the town gate" (Deut 22:15), a public place where there was space for such activity (Ruth 4:2). The office of the elders had a long history. Biblical premonarchical traditions assign them not only peaceful but also military responsibilities (Josh 8:10; 1 Sam 4:3).[39] Other leaders of the greater community in premonarchical times were known as *šôpəṭîm* (sg. *šôpēṭ*, translated as "judge"), and they also engaged in military as well as judicial activities (Deborah, Judg 4:5; Samuel, 1 Sam 7:15–17). These leaders were appointed by the elders, and their activities were limited mostly to regional matters. With the development of urban life, the office of city elders was developed following the example of village elders.

THE FAMILY

The nuclear family was the cornerstone of Israelite society in general and in village society in particular, but since the economy demanded large human resources the nuclear family joined with others in a larger unit, the extended family (*bêt ʾāb*), which sometimes included up to three generations.[40] The extended family included the (grand)father, (grand)mother, their unmarried daughters, their sons (married and unmarried), and their sons' wives and children. All of these lived in one four-room house or in a complex made of several attached houses. In addition, the compound housed unrelated people who were considered part of the extended family, including slaves, hired hands, and others (see Judg 17–18). The population of a village could be made of one *bêt ʾāb* or more. This social unit was known as a *mišpāḥâ*.[41] A person was identified by his father's lineage going back as far as five generations (e.g., Saul, 1 Sam 9:1). Familial responsibility went back as far as ten generations (Deut 23:2–9 [Eng. 23:1–8]).

Unlike urban life, village life in Iron Age I and II was directed mainly at securing the survival of the family. All efforts were made to achieve this goal. Every member of the family participated in the endeavor to survive and propagate. Men, women, and children contributed to the general welfare of the social group and its preservation. Although biological limitations determined the level of involvement, no one escaped participation. Some roles were gender-related, as mentioned in 1 Sam 8:11–13, where the males are depicted as engaged in military activities, plowing and harvesting, and manufacturing weapons, the women in baking, cooking, and making perfume.[42] This of course does not include the whole list. Many times there were crossovers between gender roles. Women helped with agricultural chores such as harvesting and sifting the grain (Ruth 2). Until their marriage, women participated in herding, as seen from the patriarchal stories (Gen 29) and the story of Moses (Exod 2:16–19). Women also had the primary responsibility for the children's education, while the men were supposed to enlist in the militia during times of need.[43]

HOSPITALITY

Hospitality was one of the most important customs observed throughout Israelite society. Actually, one might look at hospitality as a cornerstone institution of Israelite culture. There is no reason to assume that this was uniquely Israelite, but other cultures did not leave records of this practice.

It is the biblical record that reflects the practice of hospitality in a variety of ways and circumstances.

Hospitality was considered a very old custom. The patriarchal stories have several examples of hosting guests or strangers in a resplendent way. Abraham, the eponymous father of the nation, is credited with hosting divine messengers in a lavish way. He invited them to sit under a shady tree next to his tent, offered water to wash the dust off their feet, had a special meal cooked for them (bread, veal, butter, and milk), and personally made sure that they ate and enjoyed their meal (Gen 18:2–8). That this was a family custom is enhanced by the story related to the destruction of Sodom in which the same treatment was offered by Abraham's nephew Lot, who extended an invitation to the divine messengers to come to his home, where water was offered to wash their feet and a great feast in their honor was prepared. The tradition was breached by the behavior of the Sodomites, against whom Lot had to defend his guests (Gen 19:1–11). The need to protect the guests is emphasized in the story of the concubine in Gibeah (Judg 19), which is related to the period of the settlement. Here, as in the case of Lot, the Ephraimite host was willing to put the life of his family in danger to protect his guests. The rape of the concubine by the people of Gibeah, who were Benjaminites, enraged the rest of the Israelites and drove them to fight the Benjaminites. Furthermore, the Israelites were so enraged at this breach of tradition that they took a vow not to intermarry with anyone who belonged to the tribe of Benjamin (Judg 21).

That hospitality in rural Israel was an expected custom again plays an important role in the story of Gideon's call to leadership (Judg 6:11–21). Similarly to Abraham, "Gideon went (into the house) and prepared a kid and unleavened bread from an ephah of flour; he put the meat in a basket, and the broth he put in a pot, and brought them to him under the oak and served them" (Judg 6:19). In both cases, that of Abraham and that of Gideon, the end of the meal marked the appropriate time for making a transaction. The rewards and punishment for carrying out this custom are expressed in many stories. It can also be surmised that Nabal the Carmelite died because of his inhospitable treatment of David and his men (1 Sam 25).

That the custom of hospitality was practiced not only by Israelites but was part of ancient Cannan's *Sitz im Leben* (setting in life) is reflected in the biblical story of Rahab and the Israelite spies. When the spies sent by Joshua came to Jericho, Rahab hosted them and protected them against the locals who wanted to capture them (Josh 2:1–8). Protection of guests, which was emphasized in the stories of Lot and the concubine in Gibeah, is also the background of the encounter between Jael and Sisera (Judg 4:17–22; 5:24–27). Sisera, the commander of the army of Jabin king of

Hazor, was defeated by the Israelites. Escaping from the battlefield, he sought shelter in the tent of Jael, wife of Heber the Kenite. He trusted her to protect him, and she lured him in by performing several acts of hospitality. However, after he fell asleep, she killed him. Although her act was very much against hospitality protocol, she was lauded by the Israelites because they gained from this act. Another instance of hospitality by a non-Israelite is depicted in 1 Kgs 17:8–16, where the prophet Elijah enjoys the hospitality of a woman from Zarephath. In this case, the woman was able to host the prophet because of his miraculous help.

Hospitality persisted and was a strong institution in rural Israel also during the time of the monarchy. A good example is the way the Shunammite woman treated Elisha (2 Kgs 4:8–11). Whenever he passed through town, the woman invited Elisha in for a meal. After a while, when it became a habit, she allocated a portion of the house for his use. The spirit of hospitality during the time of the monarchy is reflected in many of the surviving stories from that period, one of which is the hosting of Mephiboshet son of Jonathan in David's house on a permanent basis (2 Sam 9). Another is the invitation by Hezekiah to the people of the northern kingdom to celebrate the Passover in Jerusalem (2 Chr 30). Whether real or imagined, such stories could be told since Israelite culture had a strong tradition of hospitality.

RELIGIOUS PRACTICES

Until the reforms by Hezekiah in the last quarter of the eighth century B.C.E. and by Josiah in the last quarter of the seventh century B.C.E., religious observances were family centered and took place in family shrines and in local, regional shrines. Shrines were scattered throughout the country from Dan to Beer-sheba, and the Israelites worshiped a variety of deities, including Baal, Asherah, YHWH, and others. Shrines were located on hilltops, as told in the story of Saul's first anointment (1 Sam 10:5–6, 10–13), and inside homes. Biblical references describe some of these local and regional shrines (1 Sam 1), and archaeological evidence supplies some illustrations. A village shrine supervised by one family is described in the story of Gideon (Judg 6:24–32), enumerating the different elements that were incorporated in the shrine, such as a stone-built altar and an Asherah pillar. The existence of house shrines is illustrated by the story of Micah (Judg 17–18), who built his own shrine and employed a Levite to maintain it. The existence of house shrines until at least the end of the eighth century B.C.E. is demonstrated by the discovery of such a shrine inside a domestic structure at Tell Halif.[44] The shrine was identified by its cultic paraphernalia and the head of a pillar figurine found lying on the floor.

That the Israelites worshiped deities other than YHWH is evident not just from biblical references but also from archaeological and paleographic evidence. The temple at Arad with its two standing stones in the holy of holies and the inscriptions from Horvat Taiman (Kuntillet ʿAjrûd) and Khirbet el-Qom, which mention YHWH and his Astarte, strongly suggest that YHWH had a consort named Asherah.[45] The numerous clay "pillar figurines" depicting a female supporting her large breasts with her hands that have been found in many settlements identified as Israelite confirm this notion (see fig. 2.5).

Cultic celebrations were seasonal and were determined by the appropriate occasion, such as the beginning or ending of field-crops harvest, the concluding the ingathering of fruit, the shearing of the sheep, the celebration of the new moon, and others.[46] This is well illustrated by David's excuse to abstain from King Saul's feast while celebrating with his family (1 Sam 20) and by the shearing celebrations initiated by Nabal the Carmelite (1 Sam 25) and by David's son Absalom (2 Sam 13:23–28).

THE ECONOMY

Unlike urban life, village life in Iron Age I and II was directed mainly at securing the survival of the family. All efforts were made to achieve this goal, and it was reflected in an economical system that was family centered.[47] The means of production were owned by and remained in the family, and this was true whether the economy was pastoral or agrarian oriented.[48] These and other factors, such as the inhospitable environment,[49]

Fig. 2.5. An array of pillar figurines. Courtesy The Israel Museum, Jerusalem.

critically determined the nature of the family units that constituted the village settlements.[50]

Village economy was based on seasonal work centering on tilling the
land and herding; however, men and women were engaged in many
other tasks in the off-season periods. These included production of
goods and repair of tools and installations. While the length of the workday was from sunrise to sunset, many times the day started and ended
earlier and later than that because of the need to maximize the use of
daylight (Prov 31:15). This happened mostly in seasons of fieldwork,
when the workers would leave the house in time to be in the field or
orchard at daybreak. They would remain in the field until the last possible moment. The need to exploit daylight for work, thus forcing the
workers to travel to and from the workplace in the dark, dictated the distance at which the fields or orchards were located. Beyond a certain
distance, the workers would prefer to stay overnight in the field rather
than spend long hours traveling.[51]

AGRICULTURE

Once the Israelites established their presence in the land, agriculture
became their main source of livelihood. Ideologically, the land belonged
to YHWH, and the transfer of the family plot of land (naḥălâ, ʾaḥuzzâ)
could be performed legally only through inheritance. Because of certain
economic conditions, a landowner who was not doing well could be
forced to transfer his land to another owner, but for not more than fifty
years. At the end of that period, the land would revert to the original
owner (Lev 25:8–55).[52] However, while this law was on the books, there
is no indication as to what degree it was adhered to or not. That the right
to the family plot was maintained even under harsh conditions is emphasized by the story of the Shunammite woman who was told by Elisha to
migrate to the land of the Philistines during a drought. Upon her return
after seven years, her claim to the land was recognized, and she reclaimed
her field and the value of the yield from her field during the time of her
sojourn (2 Kgs 8:1–6). There is one hint that this law was practiced as late
as the Babylonian invasion in the sixth century B.C.E. with the story of the
symbolic act by the prophet Jeremiah, who redeemed the land belonging
to his relative (Jer 32:6–44). Jeremiah, a Benjaminite from the village of
Anathoth, followed the accepted procedure of redeeming a plot of land
located in Anathoth that belonged to his cousin Hanamel. His act preserved the land in the family.

As time went on and modes of agricultural production were improved,
a surplus of agricultural produce and by-products was created. This
enabled the development of the monarchical system, which relied heavily
on taxes that were paid from the surplus.

LAND USE. Topographically and geologically, the Land of Israel is mostly hilly and rocky.[53] In addition, large parts of the country are arid or semiarid. All these harsh conditions forced the Israelites to develop special ways to overcome the environmental constraints. Part of the adaptation to these inhospitable conditions was the adoption and popularization of methods heretofore not used on a large scale. These included forest clearing, terrace building, and the practice of runoff agriculture. By clearing the forest, new tracts of land became available in the hill country. This, in addition to constructing terraces on the hilly slopes to create leveled plots of land, opened the central part of the country to settlement in areas that were previously either unsettled or hardly occupied.

Another way of gaining new agricultural land was by practicing runoff farming. This method utilized channels and check dams for the collection of rainwater off the slopes of hilly terrain and for diverting it to the terraced fields and cisterns. The method was used mostly in areas with a limited amount of precipitation to facilitate settlement in inhospitable regions such as the Negev. Most of the Negev settlements were located along trade routes, which suggests that they were prompted by the central government in order to protect the routes and the borders.

THE CALENDAR. The Israelite calendar was determined by the seasonal chores and included feasts to celebrate these events. However, the calendar presented in the Bible is actually the end result of a combination of more than one calendar, a process that took place over a long period. The biblical calendar includes remnants of the Canaanite, Israelite, and Babylonian calendars, which were introduced in different periods and under various circumstances. However, daily life was determined by the seasons and the related chores that had to be performed then. For tilling the land, we have one document, the Gezer Calendar, that helps us reconstruct the agricultural year. Discovered at the site of ancient Gezer at the beginning of the twentieth century during the excavations undertaken by R. A. S. Macalister, this inscribed limestone palette contains seven lines in which eight agricultural chores are outlined.

The Gezer Calendar reads as follows:[54]

1	two months of ingathering (olives)/ two months
2	of sowing (cereals)/ two months of late sowing (legumes and vegetables)
3	a month of hoeing weeds (for hay)
4	a month of harvesting barley
5	a month of harvesting (wheat) and measuring (grain)
6	two months of grape harvesting
7	a month of ingathering summer fruit

Since four of the chores are listed as lasting two months each, with the other four lasting one month each, they total twelve months and cover the full year.[55] The chores are planting (cereals), late planting (legumes and vegetables), weeding, harvesting cereals and grapes, and ingathering other summer fruit, including olives. The periods allotted to each chore also included sufficient time for processing and producing by-products. Israelite festivals were determined by the initiation or completion of these chores.

Sowing of cereals, which took place from late October to late December, marked the beginning of the agricultural year. (Sowing was accompanied by plowing.) This was followed by late sowing of legumes (late December to late February) and by weeding (March). Barley harvesting (spring equinox to late April), the commencement of which was celebrated with the *maṣṣôt* (Passover) festival, signaled the beginning of ingathering. Following was the harvesting of wheat (late April to late May), which ended with the celebration of *šābū̒ôt* ("weeks"; Pentecost). Grapes were harvested in June and July, other summer fruit in late July to late August, and the ingathering season concluded with two months of olive harvesting (late August to late October) which ended with the great festival of *᾿āsîp* ("ingathering"; Tabernacles).

There is nothing similar to the Gezer Calendar for chores related to herding, but since the nature of herd animals has not changed since biblical times it is possible to reconstruct the calendar of the herding population.

FIELD CROPS, FRUIT TREES, VEGETABLES, AND MORE. Israelite agricultural practices combined the richness of the country (see Deut 8:7–10) and the traditional know-how of its inhabitants. Cereals were the main field crops cultivated by the Israelites. These included wheat, barley, and millet; all were used for baking bread and other goods and for cooking porridge, gruel, and other such dishes. Barley was also used in the production of beer. The second most common group of field crops was legumes, including peas, chickpeas, grass-peas, broad beans, and fenugreek. The Israelite farmer also cultivated flax, sesame, and several kinds of spices, including dill, cumin, black cumin, coriander, and others.

Harvesting field crops integrated several other chores, such as threshing and winnowing, the end result of which was the separation of grain from the stalks and chaff. There were several methods of threshing; the choice depended on the particular crop that had to be threshed. Threshing could be done by a sledge, cart, and flailing with a stick. Winnowing was done by using a wooden pitchfork and a hoe, with the help of the wind, which separated the chaff and straw from the grain. The final cleaning was done with different kinds of sieves. The clean grain was then stored either in jars, storage pits, or in other storage facilities. In the time of the monarchy, grain was also used for paying taxes.

The main fruit trees cultivated by the Israelite farmer were grape vines and olive trees. These trees were cultivated in vineyards and olive groves, respectively, while other fruit trees such as figs, pomegranates, dates, sycomores, carobs, and black mulberries, as well as pistachios, almonds, and walnuts, were grown in smaller numbers in mixed groves not far from the house. The main product of the vine was wine; olives were grown for oil.[56] Both of these products were produced in special installations (winepress and olive press, respectively) as part of the harvesting season. The end products were stored in jars for local use, for barter, and for tax payments. The latter is well attested by the Samaria ostraca, which record the quantities of oil and wine received at the collection center in Samaria. Biblical and extrabiblical references indicate that there were different types and grades of wine and oil.

Besides eating fresh fruit in season, the Israelites used fruits to produce raisinlike dried fruit and jamlike products. Scholars suggest that the term *dəbaš* (honey), mentioned time and again in the Bible (e.g., Exod 3:8), refers many times to this product, especially the kind made with dates. Because of their high sugar content, fruits such as dates and pomegranates were also used to produce alcoholic beverages. The processing of fruits was necessary because of their short "shelf life" before spoilage. Processing fruit assured the farmer that the entire yield could be utilized without spoilage before the new harvest was ready for ingathering.

Vegetables were also cultivated, but the written and archaeological evidence is meager. Vegetables have a short growing season and had to be consumed fresh, since they could not be processed and preserved for future use. Biblical references to vegetables are few; the most famous is Num 11:5, which mentions the kinds of vegetables that were grown in Egypt. The difference between Egyptian horticulture and conditions in Canaan is further emphasized in Deut 12:10, which states that Canaan "is not like the land of Egypt ... where you sowed your seed and watered it with your feet, like a garden of vegetables." Egyptian vegetables that were also grown by the Israelite farmer included cucumbers, water and muskmelons, leeks, onions, and garlic. Farmers also cultivated gourds, especially bottle gourds (calabash). In their gardens they also grew mint and marjoram.

HERDING

Herding was the Israelites' second most important occupation. During certain periods and in certain areas, herding was the leading occupation.[57] Although herding is commonly perceived as being nomadic, Israelite herding was of the transhumant (seminomadic) and sedentary types. This means that shepherds led their animals on seasonal grazing expeditions along a prescribed circuit within a given territory while maintaining a home base or they were part of a village community that was involved in herding to a limited extent mostly for its own consumption.

Herd animals included goats and sheep, most likely black goats and fat-tail awassi sheep. Goats are hardier than sheep and are more numerous in arid and semiarid zones. Both were raised for their ability to provide milk and meat. In addition, goats provided hair, which was used in weaving tent cloth and sacks; sheep provided wool, which was used in weaving garments. Their skins could also be used for multiple purposes such as making containers for liquids (water, wine, milk), belts, footwear, and more. During and following the lambing season (December/January–June/August), sheep and goats produce milk that can be processed into several products. Although milk can be consumed fresh, without refrigeration it does not keep for long and needs to be processed for long-term use. The most common dairy products were yogurt, butter, and several kinds of cheese, the most common of which was dry cheese. Although not a herd animal, the cow was also raised for its milk and for its hide, but mostly for its muscle. All animals were kept as a source of dung for soil enrichment and for fuel.

Other animals in the Israelite menagerie included donkeys, bulls, camels, mules, and horses. These were used as draft animals. Donkeys were the most common animal used for transport of humans and cargo; camels, which were introduced relatively late, were used for transport in arid regions. Bulls (or oxen) were used as draft animals for plows and wagons. Mules were used for hauling cargo but were also considered prestigious animals. The horse was also considered a prestigious animal and was used mainly for military purposes.

While pigeons were probably kept under some controlled conditions, chickens appeared on the scene from Southeast Asia only toward the end of the monarchical period. When available, fowl provided the Israelites with another source of meat and with eggs.

OTHER PROFESSIONS AND OCCUPATIONS

Many of those who were engaged in agriculture and herding had the knowledge and talent to be involved with other occupations, which produced goods for self-consumption or barter. In the village, most of those people were engaged in them in their spare time between seasons. During monarchical times, especially in the city, when not everyone lived off the land, these occupations became professions, and their practitioners were members of guilds and maintained the know-how in the organizations and in the family circle.

POTTERY MAKING. Pottery is the art of making objects out of clay, which is later baked and hardened with heat. Since its invention in the final stages of the Neolithic period, pottery making was an activity taught by one generation to the other. As with other trades, many secrets were involved, secrets that could not be divulged. Some of them pertained to the sources of clay, the correct mixture of ingredients, the correct fashioning of the vessels, firing techniques, and more. The standardization of the vessels suggests that pottery making was in the hands of professionals a long time before the appearance of the Israelites.[58] Besides nonutilitarian objects such as figurines, most vessels were produced for daily use.

Israelite familiarity with pottery production is evident from several biblical references to the potter, his work, and his products. The image of YHWH as a potter (yôṣēr, Gen 3:7, 19; Isa 29:16; 64:8) enhances this notion and illustrates the Israelites' high regard for potters. Furthermore, several of the prophets describe the process: Jeremiah reports visiting a potter's workshop, where he sees the artisan using a potter's wheel (Jer 18:3). Second Isaiah, when he refers to Cyrus and his victories (Isa 41:25), likens him in his speeches to the potter treading the clay, and 1 Chronicles mentions the potters' guild (1 Chr 4:23).

Potters would specialize in making certain vessels and mass produce them. They would sell, barter, or exchange them in local or more distant markets. Palestinian potters produced mostly utilitarian vessels such as cooking pots, storage jars, bowls, and other kitchen vessels. In many instances neutron-activation and other petrographic analyses allow scholars to identify the source of the clay used in making a vessel. This helps in understanding economic relationships between the find site and the vessel's place of origin. Residue analysis, done mostly with storage vessels, can determine the use of the vessel. Through residue analysis it is possible to identify the contents of the vessel in antiquity, be it wine or oil.

Pottery was quite important in everyday life. Some broken vessels were mended by running a string through holes drilled along both sides of the break. Potsherds could be reused for mundane purposes such as carrying hot coals or water (Isa 30:14), for scratching an itch (Job 2:8), or for writing letters and receipts, as in the case of the Lachish letters and Samaria ostraca. Broken pottery pieces were also used by the prophets as symbolic subjects (Isa 45:9; Jer 19:10–11; Lam 4:2).

WEAVING. The term *weaving* refers to the production of fabric by interlacing two sets of yarn so that they cross each other at a right angle. A preliminary activity is spinning, which is the process of drawing out fibers from a mass and twisting them together to form a continuous thread of yarn. The large numbers of loom weights, spindle whorls, and other weaving tools in domestic contexts indicate that weaving was a major occupation among the Israelites. Ethnographic studies show that two types of looms have been in use in the Near East: the horizontal ground loom and the upright warp-weighted loom. Not much is known of the use of the former; however, the large number of Iron Age sun-dried clay loom weights found in excavations suggests that the warp-weighted loom was more common.[59] This loom type was made of a crossbeam supported by two upright beams with the warp strings tied to the crossbeam at one end and held taut by loom weights tied to their other ends.

The most common materials for making fabrics were wool and flax (Lev 13:47–48). Goat hair was also used for making tent fabric, coarse mantles, and sackcloth. That yarn was produced at the same site where weaving took place is indicated by the large number of spindle whorls also uncovered in excavations. These objects were made of different materials, such as rounded broken pottery sherds with a hole in the middle for the spindle, clay (like the weights), or bone. Although flax was grown in Palestine,[60] sheep's wool was the preferred weaving material (Ezek 34:3). Wool was used for payment of tribute, as is indicated in the Bible (2 Kgs 3:4) and in Assyrian documents. Archaeological finds show that during the period of Assyrian domination certain villages and towns specialized in weaving.

Traditionally, weaving was a woman's job (Prov 31:13, 19), although sometimes men were also involved in this activity (Isa 19:9). The different sizes of the loom weights strongly suggest that different types of fabrics were woven. Bone spatulas discovered in archaeological excavations imply that Israelite weavers were familiar with pattern weaving. This is corroborated by several references to weaving with gold and silver threads (Exod 39:3) and by references to dyed fabrics (Judg 5:30).

Dyeing is the process of adding pigment through hot or cold treatment. With textiles, the most efficient way is to dye the yarn rather than the cloth. Pigments used in dyeing come from animals, plants, and minerals. Most of these sources were available to anyone who was interested in dyeing, with one exception, the purple dye. The latter was a costly and secretive process utilizing certain mollusks (*Murex*) that became the monopoly of the Phoenicians. The high price of purple-dyed textiles contributed to the fact that it became a symbol of high status, especially royalty.

TANNING. The term *tanning,* called *reddening* in Hebrew and Greek, refers to the process of making skins and hides into soft, pliable leather. Egyptian texts and painting describe it: hides were cleaned of hair and other matter and placed in a special solution of plant juices, lime, bark, or leaves. The odor and treatment of unclean material meant that professional tanners were held in low regard. However, this process was important to make possible the use of skins and hides of slaughtered animals. One reason for raising animals was to harvest their skins for the production of clothing, footwear, belts, and containers for liquids. Ethnographic observations show that tanning has been done to a large extent as a cottage industry, and it is likely that many Israelites engaged in this process for their own needs. The process of tanning has to begin as close to the slaughter of the animal as possible; otherwise, the skin starts to decompose.

In the description of the construction of the tabernacle, tanned skins are mentioned among the offerings (Exod 25:5; 26:14; 35:7, 23). They were used in constructing covers and divisions. Having skins for an offering strongly suggests that the Israelites were familiar with and practiced tanning.

CARPENTRY. From information available in the Hebrew Bible, it appears that early Israelites were not skilled in complex woodworking, since Solomon had to import woodworkers from Tyre for the construction of the temple (1 Kgs 5:20 [Eng. 5:6]). Intricate woodworking such as making furniture and inlaying them with ivory carvings remained in the skilled hands of Phoenician artisans. However, Israelites worked with wood when they needed it for house construction. It seems that they could fell trees and shape them as load-bearing beams in building their houses. They must have used the same techniques when shaping wood for installations such as looms and when constructing simple objects such as ladders, plows, and other agricultural tools. Isaiah's detailed description of the carpenter (*ḥaraš ʿēṣîm*) and his tools (Isa 44:13) suggests that during monarchical times the Israelites became more familiar with and involved in carpentry. This is highlighted by the fact that carpenters were among the exiled to Babylon (Jer 24:1; 29:2).

MASONRY. The geology of Palestine dictated that masonry for the Israelites involved the building of structures with stones and sun-dried mud bricks. Similarly to carpentry, certain skills related to stoneworking, such as dressing stones, were unfamiliar to the early Israelites. They built their houses using fieldstones in the foundations and lower courses, with most of the superstructure made of mud bricks. Fieldstones were also used in the construction of the terraces that enabled the Israelites to settle in the hill country. At the beginning of the monarchical period, skilled masons familiar with the art of stone dressing were imported from Phoenicia by David (2 Sam 5:11; 1 Chr 14:1) and Solomon (1 Kgs 5:32 [Eng. 5:18]). Archaeological evidence indicates that, judging from the style and techniques, Phoenician involvement in Israelite construction projects continued during monarchical times. However, biblical evidence suggests that when the temple in Jerusalem was repaired, it was done by Israelite artisans (2 Kgs 12:12; 22:6; 2 Chr 24:12).

The existence of Israelite cemeteries containing manmade burial caves and cisterns carved in bedrock strongly suggests that the art of

hewing spaces in bedrock was well entrenched in Israelite society from
early times.

METALLURGY. Biblical tradition maintains that Israel did not have metallurgi-
cal know-how or that it was forced not to practice it during its early days.

> There was no blacksmith [ḥārāš] throughout all the land of Israel, for the
> Philistines said, "The Hebrews must not make any swords or spears." So
> all the Israelites had to go down to the Philistines to sharpen their plow-
> shares, mattocks, axes, and sickles. And the charge for sharpening was
> two-thirds of a shekel [pîm] for plowshares and mattocks and one-third
> of a shekel for the axes and for setting the goads. So when war broke out
> neither sword nor spear was to be found in the possession of the people
> following Saul and Jonathan; only Saul and Jonathan had them. (1 Sam
> 13:19–22)

Scholars still debate whether this passage indicates that the Philistines
had a monopoly over the production of iron tools, prohibiting the Israelites
from their manufacture, or that they were the ones who introduced iron
forging into Canaan. Archaeological evidence, including crucibles, furnaces,
and slag, suggests that already during the early days of the Israelite period
the Israelites were acquainted with metallurgy and were busily producing
bronze implements even in the outlying villages.[61] However, working with
iron is different from and harder than working with bronze, and it is possible that Israelite metallurgists were prevented by the Philistines from
learning the new technology until King David subdued them.

As with other professions, biblical tradition assigned to metallurgy its
eponymous ancestor: "Zillah bore Tubal-cain, the master of all coppersmiths and ironsmiths" (Gen 4:22). The linguistic association of the Kenites
with Cain has suggested that they were metallurgists; their long-standing
association with the Israelites (e.g., Judg 4:11; 5:24) further suggests that
they were responsible for the introduction of the Israelites to metallurgy.
Since the Kenites were a wandering people, they might have served as itinerant smiths visiting towns and villages and earning their keep in part by
smithing. The Israelites might have learned metallurgy from sources other
than just the Kenites. Egyptian written and artistic documentation indicates
that metallurgy was a well-known occupation in Egypt, and this could have
been another source for Israelite involvement in this endeavor. Space does
not allow the presentation of other possibilities for the introduction of metallurgy into Israel. Nevertheless, the Hebrew Bible is laced with evidence of
the Israelites being involved in different types of metallurgy.

That Israelites were engaged in the making of metal idols is evident
from several sources. While the story of the golden calf might be considered a myth, references to the production of metal idols (Deut 27:15; Isa

44:12; Hos 13:2) show that the story has some reality behind it. Although its makers are unknown, the early Iron Age bronze bull from the Bull Site in the Samaria hills[62] is a good example of such an idol, and there are several other examples of metal figurines from Israelite contexts.

Smithery is described in several places in the Bible where many terms related to forging, casting, beating, overlaying, furnishing, whetting, cutting, and soldering are mentioned (Isa 1:25; 48:10; 54:16; Jer 6:29; Mal 3:2–3; Ps 12:7). Furthermore, biblical references mention different kinds of smiths: silver and gold (Isa 40:19; 41:7; 46:6), iron (Isa 44:12), and bronze (1 Kgs 7:14). Metal smithery is connected with the tabernacle and temple building (Exod 36:14, 19; 39:34; 1 Kgs 7). That metallurgy became an important profession in monarchical Israel is suggested by the mention of metal smiths among the people exiled to Babylon (2 Kgs 24:14; Jer 24:1; 29:2).

WARFARE: THE EARLY YEARS

It might not seem appropriate to discuss warfare in this context, but war and peace were important factors in daily life and in the state of the economy before and during the monarchy. Israelite traditions reflect constant preoccupation with the issues of war and peace. In general, war was such a common occurrence that, as far as the Bible was concerned, specific references to times of peace became necessary. Whatever really happened in Canaan during the premonarchic period of the settlement, the Israelite mind considered that era as one of turbulence, and particular statements such as "Thus the land was at peace for forty years" (Judg 3:11) were necessary to reflect certain peaceful occurrences during the time of the judges. The same situation was prevalent when David was absorbed in establishing the first Israelite territorial state. This is well reflected in the statement attributed to Solomon: "But now on every side Yhwh my God has given me peace; there is no one to oppose me, I fear no attack" (1 Kgs 5:18 [Eng. 5:4]). However, the period of the monarchy was also marred with many wars to the point that when there was a "window" of peace it received a special mention: "and in his time [of Asa] the land had peace for ten years" (2 Chr 13:23 [Eng. 14:1]; see also 14:4–6 [Eng. 14:5–7]).

So what do we know about warfare during the early days of Israel? This will cover also the early days of the monarchy, since in that period Israelite military practices were not much different than what they were during the period of the settlement.[63] In spite of its questionable reliability, the Bible is our major source of information for these matters in the period under discussion. There are extrabiblical sources, mostly Egyptian, for the period just before the arrival of the Israelites and their rivals the Philistines in the land of Canaan. These include reports of military campaigns of several pharaohs into Canaan and the Amarna letters. The latter describe the political situation in Canaan during the Late Bronze Age, when Egypt was in control of the region. There are no good extrabiblical references to the conflicts that took place during the period of the settlement, with one exception, the Merneptah Stela (dated to ca. 1210 B.C.E.), which describes an encounter between the Egyptian pharaoh and an entity named Israel. Since the inscription raises more questions than it answers, and since by its nature it does not provide much information about the topic of warfare in this period, it cannot be relied on to shed light on the topic at hand.

Israelite traditions record that premonarchical wars were fought on land in the open country (in the Shephelah, Josh 10:8–14; in the north, Josh 11:1–9) and against fortified cities (Josh 10:31–39; 11:12–14; Judg 9:34–55).[64] The nature of the military encounters was dictated by the makeup of the Israelite fighting forces, which were made of a militia. That is, every adult male was expected to participate when he was summoned. The militia was recruited by family and clan, and certain individuals were appointed as leaders of the units. For a time, David was a commander of one of these units (śar 'elep, 1 Sam 18:13; 22:7). The overall leaders were known as šōpəṭîm (judges). Each individual was responsible for supplying his own weapons and provisions (1 Sam 13:19–22; 17:17–18). Biblical stories from the early period depict the Israelites using weapons such as oxgoads (Judg 3:31), jawbones (Judg 14:15), slings and stones (Judg 20:16; 1 Sam 17), bows and arrows (1 Sam 20:19), two-edged swords (Judg 3:16), sheaths (1 Sam 17:51), spears or javelins (1 Sam 17:45), and helmets (1 Sam 17:38). During the period of the settlement, the average Israelite did not own iron weapons (1 Sam 13:19–22).

Although the biblical redactors try to present a picture of unity among "all of Israel," the accounts related to the period of the settlement portray a situation in which certain Israelite groups elected to participate in or sit out a conflict on the basis of their own interests, which often were related to their proximity to the skirmish. A case in point is the battle led by Barak and Deborah commemorated in Judg 5, where the participating tribes are lauded while those who chose not to join are denigrated. Furthermore, the ideal Israelite unity is shattered by the many accounts of intertribal conflicts and wars.

IDEOLOGY

Ideologically, Israel's wars were the wars of YHWH, who was considered to be a warrior (Exod 15:3).[65] This notion was not limited only to the premonarchical period (Isa 42:13; Ps 24:8). Israel's enemies were considered the enemies of YHWH (Judg 5:31; 1 Sam 30:26), which is why YHWH assisted Israel in its wars (Exod 14:13–14). One way for him to intervene on Israel's behalf was through the manipulation of natural phenomena (Josh 10:11–13; 24:12; Judg 5:4–5, 20–21). To make sure that Israel won, YHWH needed to be present on the battlefield, which could be accomplished by the presence of the holy ark (1 Sam 4). Furthermore, YHWH used Israel's enemies to punish Israel for its iniquities with war that led to destruction, servitude, and captivity (Judg 4:1–2; Isa 5:26–28). In this manner Israelite ideology explained the turn of events during the period of the judges, when there were many conflicts between the tribes and other ethnic groups. This belief was not limited to the Israelites, as the Moabite Stone erected by Mesha king of Moab (ca. 830 B.C.E.) shows. In this inscription, Mesha attributed Moab's misfortunes to the fact that "Chemosh [chief god of Moab] was angry at his land."[66] Moreover, YHWH did not limit his activities to Israel and also disciplined other nations by war (Isa 13; Jer 46:1–10).

The possibility of losing one's life in a military encounter led to the formulation of specific laws exempting certain people from military service. The book of Deuteronomy, which is considered to be a late compilation of laws, includes many laws that must have been formulated in an early period. It seems that the laws of military exemption belong to the early period of Israelite history. They state:

> whoever built a new house but did not dedicate it should go back home, for he might die in battle and another man would dedicate it. Whoever planted a vineyard but has not yet enjoyed its fruit should go back home, for he might die in battle and another man would enjoy it. Whoever became engaged to a woman and did not yet marry her should go back home, for he might die in battle and another man might marry her. (Deut 20:5–7)

Additionally, "whoever is afraid or disheartened should go back home, for he might cause the heart of his fellows to melt like his" (Deut 20:8). This exemption was honored by Gideon before his battle with the Midianites (Judg 7:3).

STRATEGY AND TACTICS[67]

Because of the damage and suffering that follow war, it was to be avoided when possible. To facilitate a peaceful conclusion to a conflict, a treaty could be signed, such as the one signed between Joshua and the Gibeonites (Josh 9:3–27). One of the conditions in the treaty was military aid in case of an attack on a party to the treaty. In the case of this treaty, this condition was put to the test when the local Canaanite city-states attacked the Gibeonites and Joshua had to come to their rescue (Josh 10).

Any act of war needs preparation. The most rudimentary step is the collection of information pertaining to the condition of the enemy, which in modern parlance is known as intelligence work. This can be achieved through spying (*ləraggēl*). The Bible contains many episodes that involve spying. According to Israelite tradition, Moses sent spies to explore (*lattûr*) Canaan (Num 13), and the information they brought back discouraged the Israelites. Another spying mission undertaken under the leadership of Moses was against Jazer in Transjordan. This one ended more successfully: "they [the Israelites] captured its villages and dispossessed the Amorites who were there" (Num 21:32). The most famous spying mission is related to the capture of Jericho (Josh 2). This case involved the sending of two men by Joshua to infiltrate the city and find out the mood of the local population. The end of this story is well known: Jericho fell, and Rahab, the woman who helped the spies, and her family members were saved.

Joshua continued to employ spies during the preparations for the attack on ʿAi (Josh 7:2–3). Bethel was captured by the house of Joseph after a local man showed the Israelite spies the entrance to the city (Judg 1:22–24). Gideon, one of the major judges, personally went on a spying mission, through which he learned of the mindset of his Midianite opponents (Judg 7:9–14). He discovered that, in spite of the great numbers of the Midianites and their allies, they were scared of him, something he used to his advantage. David also sent spies (*məraggəlîm*) to find out Saul's location (1 Sam 26:5).

Assembling the forces was done by summoning them with the help of sending messages. The most common way to transmit the summon was by the use of a *šôpār* (ram's horn; Judg 3:27; 6:34; 1 Sam 13:3). The signal must have been transmitted from one location to the other, thus notifying the Israelites of the impending battle. Not all information could be transmitted by blowing the *šôpār* or a trumpet, so messengers were sent to disperse the information. The messengers would carry the summons and a verbal explanation. Whether this was true or not, the Bible mentions that at times the call for duty was backed with the messengers' transmission of human body parts (Judg 19:29) or animal parts (1 Sam 11:7) to the different Israelite communities. Such symbolic acts tended to encourage the various tribes to join.

There must have been some training in and practicing of military skills, either by individuals or groups. When David was going to learn from Jonathan whether Saul was after him, Jonathan used his bow-and-arrow target practice as a ploy to communicate with David (1 Sam 20:18–42). Testing soldiers for their skills must have been a common occurrence. Gideon tested his soldiers by having them lap water from the brook (Judg 7:5). Although the reason behind this is not completely clear, it must have been part of a routine, since they did not object to it.[68]

An important part of the routine was consulting YHWH concerning the outcome of the engagement. It was practiced in the early days (Judg 20:27;

1 Sam 13:8–10; 28:6; 30:7–8) and was also used by the kings of Judah and Israel (1 Kgs 22:5–28). This custom was not exclusively Israelite and was practiced throughout the ancient Near East. A good example for such a practice comes to us in letters from an archive belonging to king Zimri-Lim (eighteenth century B.C.E.) of Mari (Mesopotamia). In a letter to the king, his wife brings to his attention a message received from the goddess Annunitum by an individual named Shelebum during a trance:

> O Zimri-Lim, you will be tested by rebellion. Set up, keep up posted by your side to protect you the servants and officials whom you favor. Do not go about by yourself. All those who test you, I will hand them over to you.[69]

Other ways for telling the outcome of future events were by extispicy (the examination of animal organs, especially the liver) and augury (the interpretation of the flight of birds). These were practiced by the Hittites and Babylonians. For consulting YHWH, the Israelites used the services of the priests and the prophets, who employed the ephod, Urim and Thummim,[70] dreams, and necromancy. There were, however, times that the Israelites neglected to consult YHWH, as in the case of the Gibeonites, who managed to outsmart the Israelites into making a covenant with them (Josh 9:14–15).

Being small and not well armed, the Israelite militia had to resort to tactics that would give them the upper hand. The Israelites could not withstand a head-on encounter with other armies in the open field and resorted to what is considered guerilla warfare, which they adapted to the resources and conditions available to them. One famous attempt by the Israelites at a field battle against their adversaries ended in total disaster. The Israelites met the Philistines near Eben Ha'ezer, which is not far from Aphek, near the Yarkon River on the border between the coastal plain and the northern Shephelah (see ch. 1). After their first defeat, the Israelites brought the holy ark to the battlefield. However, this ended in another disaster, and the ark was taken captive (1 Sam 4).

Being the underdog, the Israelites employed psychological warfare, which is alluded to in several of the narratives. For example, when the spies returned from scouting Jericho, they informed Joshua on the local inhabitants' state of mind, saying that "all the inhabitants of the land melt in fear before us" (Josh 2:24). Looking into the state of mind of his adversaries was behind Gideon's spying mission into the camp of the Midianites and their allies (Judg 7:15). In both cases, Joshua and Gideon utilized the knowledge they acquired through spying to their advantage: when they attacked their enemies, the Israelites performed acts that puzzled and scared them. Joshua's marching around the city with the final noisemaking (Josh 6:16) and Gideon's use of noise to surprise and stun

his enemies were follow-ups to the fact that they knew that their enemies' psychological condition was fragile.

Not being able to sustain a head-on confrontation, the Israelites
employed trickery. They did it in the battle of ʿAi by feigning defeat. When
doing so, they lured the unsuspecting inhabitants of ʿAi to leave their city
defenseless while chasing the Israelites. This enabled another force to
enter and destroy the city (Josh 8). The conquest of Bethel by the house
of Joseph (Judg 1:22–26) was also possible not because of a direct attack
but because of their ability to lure one of the local inhabitants to show
them a secret passage.

Exploiting the environment to their military advantage was another
hallmark of Israelite strategy. The war between the Canaanites under Sisera[71] and the Israelites tilted in favor of the Israelites because, as described
in Judg 5, following a torrential rain the Canaanite war chariots became
bogged in the mud.

Israelite military strategy included the use of pincer attacks utilizing
two, as in the battle of ʿAi (Josh 8), three, or four heads, as was done by
Abimelech (Judg 9:34, 43–44).[72] Another tactic was the use of ambush, as
in the battle of ʿAi (Josh 8) and in the skirmishes between the Benjaminites
and the rest of the Israelites at Gibeah (Judg 20:29–41).

Israelite tactics employed commando raids such as the one executed
by Jonathan against the Philistines (1 Sam 14:1–16) and by David against
Saul (1 Sam 26:5–12). Night attacks were another way to avoid direct confrontation. Gideon conducted a night attack on the Midianites (Judg
7:16–22), and one of Saul's raids against the Philistines was done at night
(1 Sam 14:36). Raids, not necessarily by night, were also carried out by
David (1 Sam 27:7–12; 30:1–3).

Following the custom of the day, some conflicts were decided by a
duel, as in the encounter between David and Goliath (1 Sam 17). The outcome of other conflicts was decided by the engagement of small groups,
as happened between Abner and Joab (2 Sam 2:14–15).

In some instances, the Israelites are credited with direct assaults on
cities, an act that might have involved siege. Fortifications included walls
around cities, towers (Judg 8:17; 9:46–52), and gates (Judg 9:40; 16:2–3;
1 Sam 23:7). Biblical descriptions of such assaults suggest that the
Israelites used fire to destroy fortifications and to suffocate the inhabitants seeking refuge inside, as recalled of the attacks by Abimelech on
Shechem and Tebez, both located in the Ephraim hill country (Judg
9:46–53). Some archaeologists claim that the destruction of Hazor at the
end of the Late Bronze Age was caused by the Israelites. If this suggestion is correct, then Hazor is an example of what the Israelites were
capable of doing.

RESULTS OF WAR

When the armies were victorious, the end of the war was celebrated with song and dance. Miriam celebrated in song and dance the defeat of the Egyptians (Exod 14:20–21); Deborah celebrated in song the downfall of Sisera and the Canaanites (Judg 5), while Jephthah's daughter welcomed her father with dances when he returned from warring with the Ammonites (Judg 11:34). David's victory over Goliath and the subsequent defeat of the Philistines were celebrated with songs and dances by the Israelite women. However, when Israel was defeated, there was great mourning of the dead (2 Sam 1:17–27).

One way to determine victory was by counting the dead enemies. The Egyptians used to cut off the right hand of the dead enemy and counted the hands at the end of the battle. No such mention is made in the Bible except that in one case David's military success is measured by the number of foreskins he brought back to Saul (1 Sam 18:25–27). The victorious army had the right to collect booty. The defeated enemies paid dearly for the outcome of the war: cities were burned (Josh 8:28; 11:11, 13; Judg 1:8), their land was salted (Judg 9:45), and the enemy's leaders were punished severely (Josh 8:29; 10:26–27; Judg 1:7; 7:25; 8:16, 21; 1 Sam 15:33; 17:51, 54; 31:9).

FOR FURTHER STUDY

Borowski, Oded, *Agriculture in Iron Age Israel.* Winona Lake Ind.: Eisenbrauns, 1987. Repr., Boston: American Schools of Oriental Research, 2002.

A detailed description of agricultural practices in the Israelite period. The book includes discussions about land use, plant identification, agricultural methods, processing of agricultural produce, and other related topics.

———. *Every Living Thing: Daily Use of Animals in Ancient Israel.* Walnut Creek Calif.: AltaMira, 1998.

Animals were an integral part of daily life. This book presents the use of animals in rural as well as other settings. It provides information on the cultic and secular use of animals as well as the use of wild animals for different purposes.

Matthews, Victor H., and Don C. Benjamin. *Social World of Ancient Israel 1250–587 BCE.* Peabody Mass.: Hendrickson, 1993.

A detailed treatment of Israelite social structure and roles. Among the roles discussed are elders, monarchs, priests, prophets, lawgivers, storytellers, and others.

Meyers, Carol. "The Family in Ancient Israel." Pages 1–47 in *Families in Ancient Israel.* Louisville: Westminster John Knox, 1997.

An excellent discussion of the family and its role in the rural economy of early Israel. It details the responsibilities of each of the family members and the ideology behind some of the laws and customs that affected Israelite society.

Netzer, Ehud. "Domestic Architecture in the Iron Age." Pages 193–201 in *The Architecture of Ancient Israel: From the Prehistoric to the Persian Periods*. Edited by Aharon Kempinski and Ronny Reich. Jerusalem: Israel Exploration Society, 1991.

Domestic architecture was an expression of Israelite culture reflecting ideology and the economy. This work is a good source for understanding Israelite domestic architecture and its place in the socioeconomic life of this entity.

Schloen, J. David. *The House of the Father As Fact and Symbol: Patrimonialism in Ugarit and the Ancient Near East*. Edited by Lawrence E. Stager. Studies in the Archaeology and History of the Levant. Winona Lake, Ind.: Eisenbrauns, 2001.

One of the pillars of Israelite society was its social structure, which was based on the family and its leader, the father. This book is a comprehensive treatment of the Israelite family. It not only examines family structures in the surrounding cultures and compares them with the Israelite household but also describes the architectural locus of this social element.

Stager, Lawrence E. "The Archaeology of the Family in Ancient Israel." *Bulletin of the American Schools of Oriental Research* 260 (1985): 1–35.

A ground-breaking work in understanding the Israelite family and its reflection in archaeological remains. The article interprets archaeological remains recovered in surveys in the hill country.

Zevit, Ziony. *The Religions of Ancient Israel: A Synthesis of Parallactic Approaches*. London: Continuum, 2001.

Israelite religion was not monolithic and had many elements that are either not mentioned in the Bible or have been misunderstood. This recent work is a most comprehensive and well-illustrated work on the topic. It brings into the discussion archaeological as well as written evidence from biblical and extrabiblical sources. It should be consulted by anyone dealing with Israelite religion.

3

URBAN LIFE

THE CITY

Many studies have been undertaken concerning the city in Palestine, including the reasons for its rise and fall, different elements of city planning throughout history, and types of cities during various periods.[1] My aim here is to examine the different components of life in the city during the Israelite period.

Although urbanism was a well-known phenomenon in ancient Palestine, ancient Israel's urbanism "was not a continuous and uninterrupted experience, but rather a specific constellation of social circumstances that enabled an influential elite to establish governing institutions."[2] Urbanism in Israel made its appearance with the rise of the monarchy. What differentiates the Israelite city from other types of settlement is its concentration of a large population and its lack of dependence on agriculture for its livelihood. Actually, the rise of urbanism in Israel was facilitated by the creation of a mechanism to collect agricultural surplus as taxes, which was consumed by the nonproductive segments of society such as the administration, priesthood, and military.[3] Without the ability to collect and distribute surplus, ancient Israel would have remained a small chiefdom and probably would not have lasted too long.

There were several other characteristic elements that distinguished the city. These included, for example, public buildings, a fortification system, and a water system. Until the Iron Age II, cities in Palestine were mostly independent entities functioning as city-states. During the Iron Age II, the territorial state system was introduced to the region, and the city functioned not as an independent unit but as a component within a larger, more complex system. As Herzog describes it,

> The older order of royal palace-court on the acropolis surrounded by large residential quarters was replaced by a hierarchy of administrative centres serving governmental needs. Consequently, the cities of the third urban phase [Iron Age II] were gradually filled up by non-residential structures, and vacated of most of their inhabitants. The cities were occupied

predominantly by members of the state administration. The bulk of the
population moved out of the cities into the countryside to live in villages
and farmsteads.[4]

CITY PLANNING

Many of the Israelite cities were a continuation or rebuilding of Late
Bronze Age cities occupied earlier by Canaanites, Philistines, and others.
Other Israelite cities evolved from earlier Israelite villages, while Samaria
was a newly established site. Remains of earlier occupations influenced to
a certain degree the direction in which a city's development could go.
Sometimes earlier remains hampered and limited to what extent the site
could be developed. At times, earlier remains could be reused construc-
tively in the development of the new site. Being part of a larger whole,
Israelite cities had different functions, and their size and plan illustrate their
position in the administrative hierarchy. The status of each city was not
frozen but evolved through time according to changes caused by politics
and the economy. The relationship between a city and its subordinate settlements was defined as "mother and daughters."

An early study of Israelite city plans illustrates well that the Israelite
city exhibits a certain amount of preplanning, and particular elements
exhibit the result of preplanning. These include the type of fortification and
gate constructed at the site, the integration of domestic structures with the
casemate wall to form an outer ring, the ring road found at many of the
cities, the location of public structures such as palaces and storage facilities, and more (see fig. 3.1).[5]

Cities served as administrative centers that performed tax collection,
which necessitated storage facilities, and that offered defense to its citizens
and the inhabitants of the "daughters." Being an economical hub, the city
contained a marketplace and industrial zones. It was inhabited by many
who were members of the bureaucracy and thus contained housing for the
administration, military, and other citizens. However, some of the inhabitants, especially of the lower-tiered cities, were also engaged in agriculture
and herding.

CITY TYPES. Geography and topography affected the location of the cities.
Most were built at crossroads, at a defensible position, in proximity to a
perennial water source. Its location must have also determined the hierar-
chical status of each city, and the latter dictated the efforts and resources
invested in the construction of the various components of the city.

At the top of the order stood the capital (royal) cities, with Jerusalem
as the capital of the united monarchy and later as the capital of the kingdom of Judah (south) and Samaria the capital city of the kingdom of Israel
(north). Both cities were centrally located at the time of their establishment

or when they became capital cities and were next to a major highway. Capital cities were protected by an elaborate defense system and contained palaces and other public structures. Jerusalem also housed a major religious shrine that became central after Hezekiah's reforms.

Next from the top were regional centers such as Lachish in the south, Megiddo, Hazor, Dan, and others in the north. Since the north was always richer and stronger than the south, it had many more regional centers to respond to its economical needs and the large size of its population. These well-defended cities included public structures and large storage facilities, a limited number of domestic structures, and sometimes cult centers. Regional centers were used as military headquarters and as economical hubs.

Starting during the united monarchy and lasting through the life of both kingdoms, second-tier regional centers such as Beer-sheba, Taanach, and Beth-shemesh were highly important in extending monarchical control over the local population. This was taken even further down through the

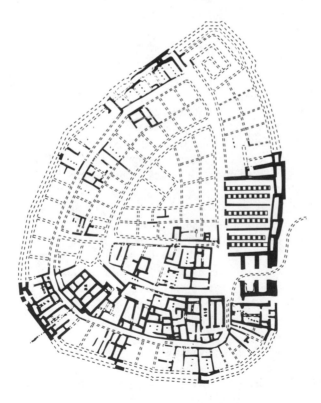

Fig. 3.1. Plan of Beer-sheba. After Ze'ev Herzog, Tel Aviv University.

provincial centers such as Gibeon, Tell Beit Mirsim, Tell en-Nasbeh, Halif, and others.[6] Through the lower-tier control centers, which can be termed towns rather than cities, the central government could exert its influence and maintain "law and order." All these cities and towns were fortified as best as the central government could afford and served an important role in the collection of taxes and distribution of commodities. The cities of the lower two tiers also contained public buildings and, where necessary, had a water system. Some of them also contained shrines.

FORTIFICATIONS. One of the most important features of any of the cities was the fortification system, which was made of several elements: city wall, ramparts, gates, towers, and more. The most important defensive element was the wall that encircled the city and presented a major obstacle for whoever wanted to overtake the site. The wall had to withstand direct and indirect assault, and this could be achieved by the type of wall and other supporting structures employed. Throughout time several types of walls were developed, and their construction depended mostly on the importance of the site to be defended and the willingness of the central government to invest in its defense.[7]

There were two basic types of defensive walls: solid and casemate walls. The solid wall was the dominant defense feature until the Iron Age, when the casemate wall was developed (see below). Nevertheless, the solid wall continued to be in use at many sites throughout the Iron Age. However, to protect the solid wall from the encroaching enemy, a series of offsets and insets was constructed to enable the defenders to protect the wall by affording them projections from the straight wall line. In some places, the offset-inset effect was accomplished by what is known as saw-tooth projections. The same effect was achieved by placing towers and bastions at critical places.

A less expensive system was that of the casemate wall, which was made of two walls running parallel to each other with, most of the time, the outer wall constructed thicker than the inner wall. Dividing walls running perpendicular to the parallel walls created rectangular spaces that could be used for a variety of activities, such as storage. In many places, such as in Beer-sheba, the casemates were actually the back room of the four-room houses adjacent to the wall and thus created an outer ring of domestic structures. Assyrian reliefs show that the walls were high and crenellated.[8]

To increase the height of the wall, at some sites a dry moat (fosse) was dug. This helped keep the attackers from rushing the wall and climbing it with ladders. This also helped keep the battering ram from being brought close to the wall. Since digging under its foundation was another way to topple the wall, it was necessary to protect its foundations. This was

accomplished by the construction of a glacis, or a sloping rampart, in front
of the wall. The glacis was constructed of beaten layers of different materials (soil, ash, stone) covered with a tightly fit layer of stones, which was
sometimes even plastered. The glacis made a direct attack on the wall and
its foundation very hard.

The weakest spot in the defense system was the gate, which was a
feature necessary to allow daily traffic in and out of the city in peacetime.
For providing access into the city without having to overcome obstacles,
the gate was usually positioned at a low spot along the wall. Although it
was an integral part of the wall, the gate was constructed as an independent defensive unit that could withstand continuous assaults. The
gate was where the battle was the fiercest, as the story about the death
of Uriah illustrates (1 Sam 11:15–18, 23–24). However, in peacetime the
gate was a center of civic activities, and its structure had to accommodate
such activities.

When discussing the gate, one should realize that this was more than
just a door; it was a gate *system*. Many cities, such as Hazor, Megiddo,
Gezer, Lachish, and Dan, had a series of gates, outer and inner, through
which traffic found its way in and out of the city. Obviously, most of the
concern was with the incoming traffic and the need to control whoever
came in and when. The road led first to the outer gate, which was placed
at a distance from the main gate. In most cases, the outer gate building had
two chambers, one on each side of the road, for guards. From there, the
road led up to the main gate; however, before the road reached the gate,
it made a turn, generally to the left. At this point, a tower or bastion protected the area. It has been suggested that the turn in the road was meant
to expose the attackers who carried their shield in their left hand to the
arrows and sling stones shot at them by the defenders from the tower.

The main gate was a formidable structure that had two or more stories
to provide space for the activities undertaken by the civic and military
administrations and by the citizenry. It could be closed at night or in times
of war by a heavy, double-winged, wooden door that was covered with
metal sheets to protect it from being set on fire. Remains of metal-sheet covers from Syria and Mesopotamia are highly decorated with mythological
scenes done in the repoussé technique. The door was bolted from the inside
with a heavy beam. The street-level floor had one to three chambers on
each side (see fig. 3.2). The gate area, including the chambers and the open
space around it, was used in peacetime for judicial, commercial, and social
activities. The city elders, as well as the king or the regional governor, met
in the gate to hold court. At Tel Dan, the remains of a low podium for an
elaborate seat and canopy were found by the gate adjacent to the open
area. The chambers in the gate at Gezer contained low benches along the
walls to provide seating, possibly for the elders or for merchants. The gate

was also an area where certain cultic activities took place (2 Kgs 23:8), as illustrated by the standing stones discovered at Dan[9] and other sites.

Some of the major cities had an acropolis or a citadel (*ʿōpel*), where the king's, or governor's, palace was located and a last stand could be mounted in case the city walls were breached and the city was invaded. Examples

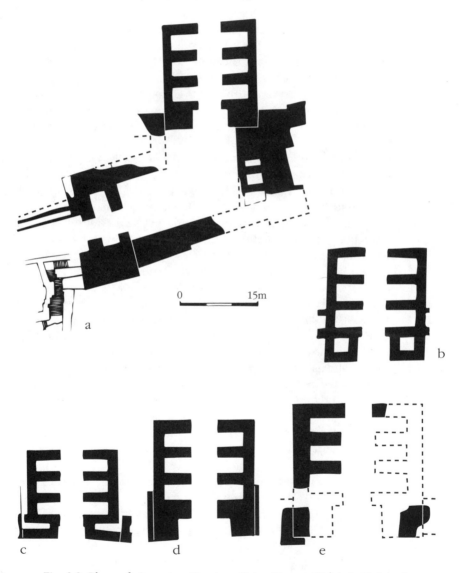

Fig. 3.2. Plans of city gates. Courtesy Ze'ev Herzog, Tel Aviv University.
a. Megiddo. b. Hazor. c. Gezer. d. Ashdod. e. Lachish.

for such a features are known from Hazor, Samaria, and Megiddo in the
north and Jerusalem and Lachish in the south.

To protect the welfare of the state, a series of forts and fortresses was
constructed along the borders and major trade routes, as for example at
Arad. These outposts were well constructed,[10] and their commander fell
under the jurisdiction of the regional governor.

WATER SYSTEMS. An integral part of the defense system was each city's water
system, since its most important function was to secure water for the city
population when an exterior source could not be reached, as in times of
war, especially during siege. Because of differences in the topography and
geological makeup, each city was forced to develop a system that relied
on the local conditions.[11] However, there were several ways of dealing
with existing conditions, as already observed in a study of water systems,[12]
which because of new discoveries is in need of updating.

According to this study, the water systems in ancient Israel can be
divided into five groups:
1. Shaft and tunnel leading to a perennial source outside the city, as
    in the third and fifth phases at Megiddo.
2. Shaft and tunnel leading to the water table within the confines of
    the mound, as at Hazor and Gezer.
3. Tunnel leading from an outside perennial source to the base of a
    vertical shaft, as in the fourth phase at Megiddo (see fig. 3.3).[13]
4. Tunnels and feeder channels diverting water (not necessarily from
    a perennial source) into reservoirs, as in Jerusalem (Siloam Chan-
    nel, Siloam Tunnel), Beer-sheba, Beth-shemesh, and Halif.[14]
5. External approach to a perennial source at the base of the mound,
    as in Megiddo (The Gallery), and Tell es-Sa'idiyeh.

To these groups should be added another one in which water was transported menially from an exterior source to an interior reservoir, as at the
Arad fortress, where water was brought to the fort from a well in the valley.

PALACES AND OTHER ACCOMMODATIONS. While domestic structures in the
cities largely continued in line with the four-room house, the new
sociopolitical structure of the monarchy dictated the necessity to develop
new types of housing for the upper classes and structures for other public needs. As described in the Bible, right from the beginning of the
monarchical period, the central authority initiated and embarked on a
huge building program that included palaces, a central shrine, and storage and military facilities. This was continued after the breakaway of the
north. "Unfortunately the very detailed specifications are for buildings in
Jerusalem, of which effectively nothing remains; while for buildings in
other localities with surviving evidence the Bible gives but cursory and

abstract reference. Thus there is little opportunity to check detail against remains so as to verify the overall circumstantiality of the literature."[15]

   Buildings are considered to be palaces ('*armôn, hêkāl, bêt melek*) based on their size, materials and construction techniques, and small finds

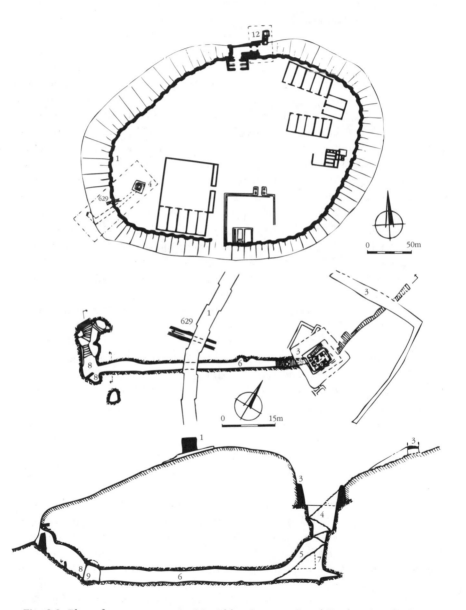

Fig. 3.3. Plan of water system at Megiddo. Courtesy Israel Exploration Society.

discovered within. Palaces housed royalty, the bureaucracy, nobility, and their entourage.[16] Based on archaeological remains and biblical references, scholars suggest that Israelite architecture was strongly influenced by the Syro-Hittite culture, with the execution done mostly by Phoenician artisans.[17] This includes the floor plan (mostly *bit hilani*), use of ashlar masonry, and integration of timber and metalwork. The term *bit hilani* refers to structures that have two elongated, parallel halls with the outer entered through a stairway leading to a doorway that stood between one to three columns. The inner room served as the throne room. It has been suggested that Solomon's palace was such a structure. Several of the Israelite palaces, such as the ones in Megiddo, included a series of rooms on the sides and back of the building. Other palaces, such as those excavated at Hazor, Ramat Rahel, and Lachish, do not follow the *bit hilani* plan but exhibit the other architectural elements mentioned above, such as the use of ashlars in the header-and-stretcher method. The official residences in the provincial cities, such as the governor's residence in Beer-sheba, are distinguished because of their size and location in the city.

In addition to ashlar masonry, another architectural element associated with royal building is the Proto-Aeolic capitals of columns found at sites such as Hazor, Dan, Megiddo, Ramat Rahel, and Jerusalem in Cisjordan and Medeibiyeh in Transjordan.[18] These capitals were identified as the "timora capitals," mentioned, for example, in 1 Kgs 6:29, 32, 35; 7:36; 2 Chr 3:5.[19]

Since taxes were paid in kind (i.e., grain, oil, and wine), their collection necessitated the construction of storage facilities. Several of the Israelite kings are credited with building such facilities; however, the biblical references do not describe them. In this case archaeology is very helpful. Many sites yielded a particular type of structure termed *pillared building* or *tripartite building*. Both designations reflect particular aspects of this structure type.[20] These rectangular buildings were divided into three elongated halls with the exterior ones paved with cobbles. Similarly to the four-room house, this structure had two rows of columns, in most cases each made out of one stone. Most scholars agree that the superstructure of this building had a roof higher over the middle aisle than over the side halls and that clerestory windows allowed light to enter. The cobbled side halls were probably used for storage of commodities in jars and other containers. At many sites tripartite buildings were uncovered in groups. Buildings of this type were excavated at Tell Abu Hawam near modern Haifa, Hazor, Megiddo, Tell el-Hesi in the Shephelah, and several other sites. These are probably the *miskənôt* mentioned in the Bible (1 Kgs 9:19 = 2 Chr 8:6; see fig. 3.4).

Other storage facilities included stone-lined, and sometimes plastered, silos that were large pits for storage of grain in bulk.[21]

POPULATION

Urbanization in Israel changed the makeup of the population in many of the major cities. Political and commercial relations brought in international elements. Marriage ties with foreign royalty and nobility introduced foreign women to the upper classes of the major cities. Political relations brought into the capital cities, temporarily or for an extended period,

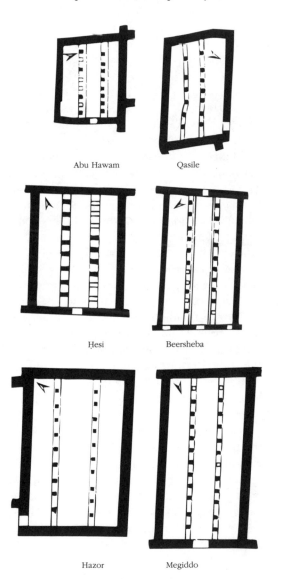

Fig. 3.4. Plans of tripartite buildings. Courtesy *Biblical Archaeologist*.

ambassadors of foreign powers. Foreign relations evolved and included international trade, which introduced a number of foreign merchants. The great wave of construction brought from the outside artisans, and the accumulated wealth created a need for luxury items, which was satisfied in part by the importations of foreign artists. To protect the monarchical order and its possessions, mercenaries were recruited from outside Israelite society. Thus the population of cities such as Jerusalem included ethnic elements such as Hittites, Amorites, Arameans, Phoenician, Egyptians, and Transjordanians (Ammonites, Moabites, Edomites, Arabs). This process, and the fact that it made the cities densely populated and expensive to live in, drove many Israelites out of the cities and into the smaller towns, villages, and homesteads. Of course, this changed the nature of life in the big cities, a process that sometimes was met with resentment and opposition.

To keep control over matters, the monarchy developed a variety of means. First and foremost was a central government, the seat of which was the capital city. The Bible gives us the list of ministers under David and Solomon (David, 2 Sam 8:15–18; 20:23–26; 1 Chr 18:15–17; 27:32–34; Solomon, 1 Kgs 4). We know from inscriptional evidence that after the division of the kingdom some of the offices were continued in the south. Unfortunately, no list such as the one mentioned above exists for the kingdom of Israel.[22] Serving the government was an administration that included scribes, commanders of the different armed forces, priests, advisors, and a tax commissioner in charge of the corvée. David was the first Israelite monarch to accumulate so much wealth that he needed supervisors to manage and control it (1 Chr 27:25–31), while Solomon could supply his household needs only by dividing his kingdom into twelve provinces, each under an official charged with the monthly provisioning of the palace. There were other officials and courtiers stationed in the capital city and in the palace. We learn of such individuals from references in the Bible, inscriptions, and seals and seal impressions, such as ʿebed (servant), ʾăšer ʿal habbayit (over the house), śar hāʿîr (mayor), and more. High public positions were not reserved only to men. Women also occupied important public positions, as we learn from the mention of Huldah the prophetess (2 Kgs 22:14) and from the seal of Maadana, daughter of the king.

Indeed, each city or town had its own governing body made of elders. The council of elders in the city was formed in a way similar to that of the village.[23] Cities and towns had liaisons with the central government. These were officials who were in charge of tax collection and drafting citizens for militia duty or for corvée work. They were also responsible to discharge commodities to certain functionaries who were paid for their services. Military units stationed in the different communities were under a local commander who was responsible to the central government, either directly or through an intermediary officer.

The new socioeconomic and political conditions created a new upper class made of the royalty, nobility, and priests. Members of this class developed a lifestyle significantly different from what the lower classes were accustomed to. For those who were concerned with social justice, it became an extremely irritating condition that found its expression in some of the prophetic speeches. Through these speeches we learn of this lifestyle of indulgence and greed, which included overeating and drinking at banquets (Isa 11–12; 21; Amos 4:1; 6:1–7) and carrying out many injustices perpetrated upon the poor, such as cheating and stealing their property (Isa 5:8; Jer 5:27–28; 22:3, 13–17; Amos 2:6–8; 5:7–12; 8:5–6).

RELIGION

Life in the city included participation in cultic practices that took place at the local shrine. From biblical references and archaeological finds it is safe to assume that every city and town had a cult center or a shrine. Some shrines were more important than others, and they are the ones mentioned in the Bible, although not all of them have been recovered in excavations. On the other hand, some shrines that have been discovered are not mentioned in written sources.[24]

The discovery of home shrines such as the one at Tell Halif[25] and at other sites suggests that family worship continued even in the urban setting. Jeremiah describes it well: "Do you not see what they are doing in the towns of Judah and in the streets of Jerusalem? The children gather wood, the fathers kindle fire, and the women knead dough, to make cakes for the queen of heaven; and they pour out drink offerings to other gods, to provoke me to anger" (Jer 7:17–18).

The makeup of the population in the large cities suggests that a large part of the cult became public. The Jerusalem temple, which began as a royal shrine and only later became a national shrine, is described in detail in the Bible, but no remains have yet been recovered. On the basis of the biblical descriptions, scholars suggest that the Solomonic temple must have been similar to the one excavated at Tell Ta'inat in Syria and to similar temples that follow the general floor plan of tripartite Syrian temples. It has been suggested that a carved ivory scepter head with an inscription reading "holy to the priests/(belonging) to the house of [YHWH]" originated in the Jerusalem temple. If true, then this is the only known remnant of the Jerusalem temple.

The nature of worship in the Jerusalem temple and at other shrines can be re-created from biblical references and archaeological finds. Reports in the Bible suggest that not only YHWH was worshiped in the temple. Because of political pressure and under the influence of foreign ethnic elements, several kings introduced modes of worship that were foreign to the Israelites. Actually, the monotheistic point of view expressed in the prophetic books was followed by only a small number of Israelites.

The Bible mentions several temples, but only the elaborate sanctuary at Dan has been discovered. At this site excavators uncovered an open cult center (*bāmâ*) made of ashlars and other religious installations and paraphernalia.[26] Other urban sites mentioned in the Bible as having cult centers yielded only religious objects but no trace of the center itself. Most famous of these is Beer-sheba, where a sacrificial altar made of ashlars was found in secondary use in the wall of a storehouse. However, the site of the cult center at Beer-sheba has not been discovered. It has been proposed that the cult center at Beer-sheba was destroyed during Hezekiah's reforms. The reforms did not eliminate cult observances in all urban centers because several urban sites yielded house shrines.

Not all regional temples are mentioned in the Bible. One of these was discovered at Arad. This temple had a long history starting in the tenth century B.C.E. and ending around 700 B.C.E. During this long period, the temple went through several changes. Generally, it follows the floor plan of a tripartite temple having an open court with a large sacrificial alter, an enclosed broadroom, and an inner sanctum, which had two *maṣṣēbôt* (standing stones) with two incense altars in front of them. It seems that the temple was taken out of service during Hezekiah's reforms.

In summary, Israelite cult practices in the urban setting continued to be celebrated as a family affair, but in many instances people took advantage of the extant public facilities either by choice or as a result of reforms instituted by the central government.

THE ECONOMY

As already noted earlier, most inhabitants of the cities did not rely for their livelihood on agriculture or herding. Most city folks were either connected with the bureaucracy or were engaged in activities that enabled the bureaucrats to function. Many city inhabitants were engaged in manufacturing activities similar to those carried out in the villages, such as pottery making, stone cutting and masonry, brick making, metallurgy, weaving, and the production of foodstuffs in large quantities for sale. The latter included bakers (Jer 37:21; Neh 3:13; 12:38); other services for sale probably included laundry (Isa 7:3; 36:2). An important component of urban economy was commerce.

TRADE AND COMMERCE

During the premonarchic period, the economy was based on self-sufficiency, with small-scale barter using limited quantities of surplus that was produced by the small landowners in the highland villages and home-steads.[27] With the rise of the monarchy, the nature of the economy changed when trade and commerce were introduced and became a major element of the economy.

When discussing commerce in ancient Israel, the following should be considered: (1) overland trade, which includes short-distance trade and long-distance trade, including desert trade; and (2) maritime trade.

Most long-distance trade was under royal monopoly or by special permits with taxes and fees exacted by the government. This helped maintain the commercial infrastructure and supported some of the financial need of the monarchy. These taxes were added to the price of the imported goods and made them luxury and prestige items. Royal Israelite involvement in trade is echoed in the biblical traditions connecting Solomon to trading in horses and chariots, his connections with the Queen of Sheba, and his maritime expeditions (1 Kgs 10:11–12, 28–29; 2 Chr 1:16–17; 8:17–18; 9:1–13).

OVERLAND TRADE. Most commerce was short-distance overland commerce; this included the movement of commodities between villages and from villages to the cities. Small markets, like the ones still being held today by and for bedouin on the outskirts of towns and the ones held on a weekly basis in European towns and villages, were held in ancient Israel. Most of the commodities and goods available in these markets were surplus and other products made by the rural inhabitants. The agricultural surplus included mostly grain, oil and wine, and livestock such as young lambs and kids. Possibly, it also included fresh fruit and vegetables in season or by-products such as dry fruit and cheese.

Most roads between villages were no more than paths following the terrain. Goods were transported mostly on donkey back, which can be considered the jeep of the ancient Near East. When the monarchy became involved in commerce and some of the roads were improved and maintained, wagons were also used in transport, with oxen serving as the main beast of burden. It is possible that mules were also used for this purpose; however, it seems that horses were not used for everyday cargo hauling.[28]

City folk could purchase their needs through middlemen, while villagers probably exchanged among themselves. Since coins were not yet invented, the exchange was made either for precious metals and stones or as barter for other goods or services. Dry and liquid commodities were measured by units of volume, many of which are mentioned in the Bible and in extrabiblical inscriptions such as the Samaria and Arad ostraca. The worth of goods and the unit of exchange were determined by weight; the unit was the silver shekel. Weighing was done with a balance scale that held the goods at one end and weights at the other. Denominations available beside that of the shekel and its multiples were also fractions of a shekel, such as *gērâ, beqaʿ, pym,* and *neṣep.*[29] While some of the denominations are known from biblical references, many details concerning the weight system are known from archaeological finds. Many weight stones, especially from eighth-century Judah, were found in archaeological excavations; they are dome-shaped, made of limestone, and in most cases carry on the top of the dome an inscribed denomination. Multiples of the shekel denomination carry a sign similar to the Greek letter gamma and a denomination numeral, some of which are in Egyptian. It has been suggested that at the end of the eighth century B.C.E. changes were made in the Judean weight system from the Egyptian *deben/qedet* to one that was more in line with the Assyrian system. Furthermore, this change was a result of growing commerce with the Assyrian Empire, while contacts with Egypt were diminished.[30] It is possible that such changes were made under King Hezekiah as part of his reforms, which included religious as well as economic reforms.

Haggling in the market over the price of merchandise is not something that only the modern tourist to the Middle East experiences upon visiting the oriental bazaar. The story of Abraham's purchase of the Cave of Machpelah (Gen 23) and Abraham's haggling over the price of saving the city of Sodom (Gen 18:17–33) are good examples of typical market behavior in biblical times.

Long-distance trade throughout the ancient Near East was not an Israelite invention. International trade was in practice from the early stages of history in the Near East, as demonstrated by objects uncovered in archaeological excavations and by written documents related to commercial activities discovered in the ancient archives of Ebla, Mari, Ugarit, and others. Furthermore, trade needs and responsibilities were included in international treaties. The Bible attributes involvement in commerce to the Canaanites and sometimes uses the term *Canaanite* as equivalent to merchant (Isa 23:8; Ezek 17:4; Hos 12:8; Zeph 1:11; Zech 14:21; Prov 31:24). Indeed, the attitude of conservative biblical circles toward trade was highly negative (Ezek 28:4–5). Traders followed established land routes. The most prominent of these was the Via Maris (the Way by the Sea), which went from Egypt along the eastern shore of the Mediterranean (hence the name) through Syria-Palestine to Mesopotamia. The main road had several branches into the hill country and other regions. Another important road, referred to as the King's Highway, ran north-south in Transjordan.

Conditions along the main road that connected major cities such as Ashkelon, Gezer, Megiddo, Hazor, Dan, and others allowed, in addition to donkeys and camels, the use of carts and wagons. The major cities had overnight accommodations for the commercial caravans as well as large open markets and enclosed stores, as shown by archaeological finds at

Dan and Ashkelon, respectively.[31] With the domestication of the camel and its introduction to the region sometime around 1200 B.C.E.,[32] desert caravans connected the eastern Mediterranean with faraway locations beyond the Arabian and Syrian deserts. The use of camels in the transport of goods, especially incense, is illustrated in the Joseph story, where an Ishmaelite camel caravan is described as carrying "gum, balm, and myrrh" (Gen 37:25). The final resting place of many of these camels is demonstrated by the finds of many carved camel bones at Ashkelon.[33] Goods imported from other parts of the ancient world found their way to local markets through intermediaries and middlemen who distributed along the local routes to the towns and villages the goods purchased at the long-distance trade terminals. Among the exotic items brought to Israel by the long-distance traders were foodstuffs that were unavailable locally and were processed and purchased at faraway places such as Egypt (e.g., fish). Other items brought by long-distance traders included jewelry, pottery vessels, and the commodities they contained.

MARITIME COMMERCE. Sea trade around the Mediterranean goes back to at least the Late Bronze Age, as shipwrecks along the southern coast of Turkey and other sites along the eastern Mediterranean indicate. Items imported from Cyprus and other parts around the Mediterranean basin illustrate the same. Maritime activity continued throughout the Iron Age under the continued dominance of the Phoenicians (Ezek 27–28), who by 900 B.C.E. set up colonies on the Mediterranean shores and on defensible promontories as far as Spain and were the seafarers of the ancient world. Their continuous involvement throughout the Iron Age II has been recently documented by the discovery of two of their ships off the coast of Ashkelon.[34] From these wrecks and from other written and archaeological evidence it appears that the main objects of Phoenician trade were grain, oil, wine, wood, and purple dye.

Maritime trade was conducted mostly along the shores; however, deep-sea sailing was seasonal because it depended on the winds and streams prevalent in certain seasons. Israelite maritime activity was closely connected to that of the Phoenicians. Biblical references to Israelites associated with sailing are limited to groups located in close proximity to the Phoenicians, such as Zebulun (Gen 49:13), Dan, and Asher (Judg 5:17). Solomon was also involved in joint maritime expeditions with the Phoenicians (1 Kgs 9:26–28; 10:11–12; 2 Chr 1:16–17; 8:17–18). These expeditions brought back gold and silver, precious stones, and exotic trees and animals. King Jehoshaphat of Judah (ca. 874–850 B.C.E.) attempted to emulate Solomon's maritime success in acquiring gold (1 Kgs 22:49); however, his ships were wrecked. King Ahaziah of Israel (ca. 850–849 B.C.E.), who wanted to make it a joint venture, was rebuffed by Jehoshaphat (1 Kgs

22:50). According to the account in 2 Chr 20:35–37, the reason for the failure of the mission was Jehoshaphat's cooperation with Ahaziah.

No other maritime activities related to Israel are reported in the Bible or can be gleaned from other sources.

WHEN THE KINGS WENT TO WAR

The rise of the monarchy in Israel prompted the rise of urbanism. This, in turn, caused a drastic change in the sociopolitical structure, which created a new lifestyle that encouraged the accumulation of wealth. The new economic conditions in Israel, on one hand, served as an attraction for outside forces and, on the other, encouraged offensive actions, all of which resulted in countless wars. In terms of warfare, the period of Saul and David was one of transition. During this period, especially in the middle and latter days of David, one can observe a slow change in the makeup of the army, the weaponry, and the strategy. Saul continued to wage mostly defensive wars because this was his stated mandate (1 Sam 8:20). It fell to David to be the first Israelite king to initiate offensive wars for the purpose of extending the territory under his control. As king, David was the first to employ mercenaries; the Cherethites and the Pelethites, originally members of the Sea Peoples coalition, were under the command of Benaiah son of Jehoiada (2 Sam 8:18; 20:23). David also employed Uriah the Hittite (2 Sam 11), who must have been a mercenary. David had a unit of special forces, a few of whom were not of Israelite origin, who participated in daring operations (2 Sam 23:8–39; 1 Chr 11:10–47; 12:1–22). David also employed Israelite units in his army (1 Chr 12:23–38).

Many of the tactics used by the Israelite tribal confederacy were maintained during the early monarchy. David continued to rely on foot soldiers, while his enemies used chariots (2 Sam 10:18). When he captured horses from his enemies, David "hamstrung all the chariot horses but left enough for a hundred chariots" (2 Sam 8:4; see also 1 Chr 18:4). It has been suggested that he did so because he had no aspirations to build a chariotry force. Spying continued to be used. Thus Hanun king of Ammon suspected David's emissaries, who came to console him after the death of his father Nahash, of being spies (2 Sam 10:3; see also 2 Chr 19:3). Duels continued to be utilized as a means to decide the outcome of the conflict (1 Chr 20:4–8). When the armies of Joab and Abner met at the pool near Gibeon, Abner suggested and Joab agreed to have the result of a series of duels decide the outcome of the conflict. Only when the result was a draw did the armies face each other in a field battle (2 Sam 2:13–17).[35]

However, efforts were made to avoid war, and David used treaties to establish relationships with his adversaries, starting with the house of Saul (2 Sam 3:12–21) and continuing with Israel's neighbors. To achieve the latter, David married the daughters of neighboring kings. This move assured him support and at times provided shelter and refuge for him and for his offspring (2 Sam 13:37–38).

Fortification systems continued to include walls and gates, as can be learned from some of the war stories. Most prominent for the early monarchical period are the stories of David's conquest of the strongly fortified Jerusalem (2 Sam 5:6–9; 1 Chr 11:4–8) and the war against Rabbah of the Ammonites. The latter is connected with the incident of David and Bathsheba, since her husband Uriah was involved in the assault on the city after a long siege (2 Sam 11–12). The conquest of Jerusalem was possible when David's forces under Joab managed to penetrate the city through the ṣinnôr, supposedly an element in the water system.[36] According to biblical accounts, when David's forces attacked Abel of Beth-maacah, where the rebellious Sheba ben Bichri had sought refuge, they besieged the city, built a siege ramp (sōləlâ), and attempted to destroy the city wall (2 Sam 20:14–15) either by ramming or undermining it. Punishing the defeated was part of the consequences of war, and in some cases the punishment was quite harsh (2 Sam 12:31; see also 1 Chr 20:3).

Solomon's time is considered by the Bible as a time of peace: "he [Solomon] had peace on all sides. Judah and Israel lived in safety, everyone under his own vine and his own fig tree from Dan to Beer-sheba, all the days of Solomon" (1 Kgs 5:4–5 [Eng. 4:24–25]). But in spite of these claims of peace, it was Solomon who introduced to Israel chariotry and cavalry on a large scale (1 Kgs 5:6 [Eng. 4:26]; 9:19; see also 2 Chr 8:6, 9; 9:25, 28), and, as the biblical text records, it was Solomon who built fortified cities on a large scale (1 Kgs 9:15).[37] It is possible that because of these efforts Solomon was successful in achieving peace for his citizenry during his lifetime. Moreover, it is possible that the pax Solomonica was a result of Solomon's insistence on treaties that were sealed by marriage, the most famous of which was his marriage to the daughter of Pharaoh (1 Kgs 3:1).

Following the division of the monarchy (ca. 920 B.C.E.), the kings continued to employ a standing army (2 Chr 17:12–19; 25:5–10; 26:11–15), fortified and refortified cities when conditions demanded it (2 Chr 17:2; 26:9–10; 27:3–4; 33:14), used chariotry (1 Kgs 22:4, 34–35 = 2 Chr 18:33–34; 2 Kgs 8:20–21), and sometimes also conducted night raids (2 Kgs 8:21). Weaponry included swords, bows, and personal armor (1 Kgs 22:34 = 2 Chr 18:33). Treaties were made and broken, and alliances continuously changed. They fought Egypt (2 Chr 12:9; 14:7–14 [Eng. 14:8–15]; 35:20–24), skirmished with the Edomites (2 Chr 25:11–14a), continued the conflict with the Philistines and other groups (2 Chr 26:6–8; 27:5; 28:17–19), fought with and against the Arameans with or without treaties with Israel (2 Chr 16:1–6; 24:23; 2 Kgs 15:16–22; 2 Chr 28:5–6), and conducted wars between the two kingdoms, Israel and Judah (2 Chr 25:17–24;

28:7–15). Ancient Israel's involvement in wars is evident also from extra-biblical sources. The Moabite Stone erected by King Mesha of Moab testifies to the territorial expansion of the northern kingdom under the Omrides even as far as southern Transjordan.[38] Assyrian annals are a good source of information for some military encounters in which Israel participated. Shalmaneser III (ca. 858–824 B.C.E.) reports that Ahab of Israel contributed two thousand chariots and ten thousand foot soldiers to the Aramean coalition he faced.[39] The latter reference, when compared with the forces contributed by the other members of the coalition, shows that Israel was a great military power.

The worst wars were those that brought the extinction of the two kingdoms. The first outside world power that confronted the Israelites was Assyria, which brought devastation to Judah and annihilated Israel (2 Kgs 15:29; 17:1–20; 18:9–17; 2 Chr 28:16–21; 32; 33:10–13). The final blow to the Israelite entity was delivered by the Babylonians (2 Kgs 24:1–2, 10–17; 25:1–21; 2 Chr 36:6–7, 10, 17–20). Both the Assyrians and Babylonians used siege techniques in capturing Samaria (2 Kgs 17:5) and Jerusalem (2 Kgs 25:1–4). Assyrian reliefs depict the impaling of rebellious leaders as punishment, and written documents such as biblical and extrabiblical records tell of the exile of the upper classes (2 Kgs 24:14–16; 25:19–21; 2 Chr 36:20). Exile, or the exchange of populations, introduced into the area new ethnic elements and new ways of thought. The economy reverted to rural and remained so for a long period.

FOR FURTHER STUDY

Biran, Avraham. *Biblical Dan.* Jerusalem: Israel Exploration Society and Hebrew Union College-Jewish Institute of Religion, 1994.

This is a popular book on an important Israelite city written by its excavator. The book covers the history and archaeology of the site from the pre-Israelite periods through the biblical period. Special topics accompanied with many illustrations are the metal industry, the sacred precinct, the Aramaic (Beth David) inscription, and more. It is a good example for what an Israelite city was like.

Herzog, Zeev. *Archaeology of the City: Urban Planning in Ancient Israel and Its Social Implications.* Tel Aviv: Institute of Archaeology, Tel Aviv University, 1997.

The most comprehensive book on the topic of urbanism in biblical Israel. It not only covers the development of the city in Palestine, the different urban phases in this area, and the ideology behind the Israelite city but also describes in detail all major cities and their history.

Reich, Ronny. "Palaces and Residences in the Iron Age." Pages 202–22 in *The Architecture of Ancient Israel from the Prehistoric to the Persian*

Periods. Edited by Aharon Kempinski and Ronny Reich. Jerusalem: Israel Exploration Society, 1992.

Public buildings and the accommodations built for and used by the wealthy are important elements of a city. This work describes palaces in the united and divided monarchies, governor residences, and materials for and techniques of construction of these structures.

Shiloh, Yigal. "Elements in the Development of Town Planning in the Israelite City." *Israel Exploration Journal* 28 (1978): 36–51.

The first major attempt to study the urban phenomenon in ancient Israel. This work, which calls attention to several architectural elements in city planning, has served as the basis for later studies.

Ussishkin, David. *The Conquest of Lachish by Sennacherib.* Tel Aviv: Institute of Archaeology, Tel Aviv University, 1982.

Lachish was a major Judahite city known mostly because of its role in Hezekiah's rebellion against Sennacherib. In this book, this event is analyzed in light of the results of the archaeological excavations and the study of Sennacherib's reliefs. The illustrations are excellent, especially for the study of the city fortifications, military techniques, and the depiction of several ethnic groups including Judahites.

Wright, George R. H. *Ancient Building in South Syria and Palestine.* Vols. 1–2. Leiden: Brill, 1985.

The most comprehensive work covering the issue of town planning and building from the Stone Age through the Persian period. Volume 1 (text) describes the background of urbanism, the nature of this phenomenon during different periods, elements of building (e.g., fortifications, temples, houses), construction techniques, and more. Volume 2 (illustrations) provides over 367 drawings illustrating the material discussed in the first volume.

4

THE HOUSEHOLD AND LIFE CYCLES

The Israelite family invested most of its efforts in making a living, whether by tilling the land, herding, or a combination of the two. Other activities were related to maintaining and improving the quality of life. These included providing shelter, food preparation, making tools and clothes, and more mundane things such as doing laundry (Jer 2:22) and similar tasks. A discussion of the Israelite household and family life revolves around several topics, including daily routine, diet and food preparation, health, family structure, life cycles, and related customs and legal frameworks.

Since not much can be done without nourishment, food will be the first matter to be discussed.

THE ISRAELITE DIET

It is assumed that the ancient Mediterranean diet was a healthy one, and many modern references are made to this effect. Although there is evidence that some of the ancient inhabitants of the region were not slim and trim,[1] most of the available information suggests that most people were not overweight, due to their diet and the strenuous physical activities in which they were engaged. In discussing the ancient diet, I assume that throughout the ancient Mediterranean world conditions were almost the same as in Palestine and the diet was very similar; therefore, materials from different cultures and sources will be consulted in the following study.

Eating well and right was always important, as implied by the Deuteronomic statement: "You shall eat, be satiated, and bless YHWH your God for the good land he has given you" (Deut 8:10). The latter reference leads us to the first topic of our investigation, food resources.

FOOD RESOURCES

The Bible considers Eretz Yisrael to be a land "flowing with milk and honey" (Exod 3:8 and elsewhere), two foods that some scholars consider to be wholesome.[2] On other occasions, the Bible considers "cereal, wine, and oil" as the main food elements. However, written and archaeological evidence indicate that the ancient menu was much more diverse. The daily menu can be divided into two groups: (1) products of field plants and fruit trees, and (2) animals and animal by-products. The Israelite menu was closely related to cultic practices because most of what was allowed as sacrifice could also be eaten, and certain foods were consumed mainly at cultic events and were not part of the normal daily diet. Therefore, an investigation of the Israelite diet should commence with the examination of the sacrificial lists.[3]

It has been suggested that "food is one of the primary symbols manipulated by people seeking to maintain their cultural identity and group solidarity,"[4] but for whatever reason we are in possession of only the Israelite detailed dietary lists. For the Israelites, food was one way for self-definition. While it is impossible to know how closely the dietary laws were observed, self-definition is most likely the basis for certain biblical lists enumerating different kinds of animals permitted or forbidden for consumption.[5] In addition, some taboos do not relate to the source of the food but to the mode of preparation, as in the case of boiling a kid in its mother's milk (Exod 23:19; 34:26; Deut 14:21). There are no lists containing forbidden plants, so we can assume that there was no prohibition against eating any plant or fruit, and the limitations on their consumption would have been dictated by taste and toxicity (2 Kgs 4:39–40) and the fulfillment of religious injunctions such as tithe.

Only native growth was considered fit for sacrifice. However, as seen from zooarchaeological studies, certain wild animals and fish were eaten but were not listed in any sacrificial list. Although some Israelites must have been engaged in fishing, this activity was probably introduced after the basis for the sacrificial lists was formed, which is the reason for fish not being listed. Since certain birds (dove, turtledove) are listed on the sacrificial lists (Lev 1:14; 5:7), we can safely assume that they, too, were raised domestically. To them, we can add as fit for food the wild quail and rock partridge.[6] The birds that could not be eaten are identified by name (Deut 14:12–18), and it seems that their common characteristic is that most of them are birds of prey and carrion eaters. As far as mammals are concerned, the general rule permitting their consumption is stated in Deut 14:6: "any hoofed animal that has cloven hoofs and also chews the cud." This definition fits well the ruminants available for the Israelites. The most common animals to be consumed, as seen from biblical references and zooarchaeological evidence, included small and large cattle, in this order. The rule for water fauna was simple: "Of all that live in water these may be eaten: whatever has fins and scales" (Deut 14:9). Creatures that "swarm on the ground" (Lev 11:29–30), such as rodents and lizards, as well as insects (Lev 11:41–44) were prohibited; however, the locust was permitted (Lev 11:20–23) and even considered a delicacy.

THE MENU

Food the Israelites consumed can be divided into two categories: daily meals and festive or ritual foods. Most of the biblical and extrabiblical sources record festive occasions and celebrations such as welcoming guests or civic and cultic celebrations. Among the latter we can count the inauguration of the temple by Solomon (1 Kgs 8:63–66; 2 Chr 7:5–9). To get an idea what might have been consumed then, one should note that Solomon's daily provisions included thirty kor[7] of fine flour, sixty kor of flour, ten fat oxen, twenty oxen, a hundred sheep, as well as stags, gazelles, roebucks, and fattened fowl (1 Kgs 5:2–3 [Eng. 4:22–23]).[8] When Ashurnasirpal II inaugurated the palace in Calah, he wined and dined 69,574 men and women for ten days.[9] It is obvious that what was eaten on these occasions was not daily fare, but these descriptions illustrate the available resources.

One example for a complete meal is that of Abraham feeding the three messengers (Gen 18:6–8). On this occasion Abraham offered cakes, a well-prepared young calf, curds, and milk.[10] Although this meal was prepared in haste and was meant for guests, it is similar to what is described in the story of Sinuhe (ca. twentieth–nineteenth century B.C.E.), an Egyptian nobleman who resided in Canaan for a time: "Bread was made for me as daily fare, wine as daily provision, cooked meat and roast fowl, beside the wild beasts of the desert, for they hunted for me and laid before me, beside the catch of my (own) hounds. Many ... were made for me, and milk in every (kind of) cooking."[11] Both Sinuhe and Abraham were members of a well to-do social class; thus, what was available to them might not have been typical. Certain descriptions in the book of Ruth will serve for comparison with the working class. During the day, the workers who were harvesting ate the following items in the field: bread, which they dipped in vinegar,[12] and parched or roasted grain (Ruth 2:14). They drank water to quench their thirst (Ruth 2:9). Quite similar to what Ruth and her cohorts ate, simple yet nourishing, is a traditional breakfast in many Middle Eastern agrarian societies, which includes pita (flat, round, "pocket" bread) dipped in olive oil, za'atar (a Middle Eastern condiment),[13] and onion.[14] Sometimes a hard-boiled egg dipped in oil or fat is added. The traditional vegetarian nature of the Near Eastern diet is well exhibited also in the typical Druze meal, which may include olives, bread, eggplant, cauliflower, chickpeas, rice, wheat, potatoes, salad, yogurt, and fruit.[15] Although some of the listed components are relatively new to the region, the vegetarian principle has been maintained.

BAKED GOODS. Cereals and legumes were the basic food elements that could be consumed in various ways. They contain a variety of minerals and vitamins highly important to maintain good health. In season, grain could be eaten fresh (whole or mashed), and when dry it could be parched or roasted for immediate consumption. Whole or cracked grain could be used in gruel (Gen 25:29, 34) and stew. Using grain in this manner is very healthy because it retains the bran and germ. However, the most versatile way of using grain is by first grinding it to flour. Grinding was done in stone mortars with pestles made mostly of stone and with grinding stones. Mortars could be portable or carved in bedrock, and grinding stones were made of a pair, with the upper rubbing against the lower while the grain was placed in between. The product was whole flour, but this flour had one flaw: it contained a high amount of grit that, when consumed, ground down the tooth enamel and the teeth themselves, thus contributing to problems with oral health.

Flour is a raw substance that can come in various grades. When mixed with liquids and spices, it can be made into different products, the most common of which is dough that, in turn, can be made into a variety of baked goods. Baked goods can be divided into leavened and unleavened. Given enough time and proper conditions, the preference would be to make leavened bread.[16] Bread was a major component of each meal; thus the same term (*leḥem*) was applied to food in general and to food processed from grain. Besides bread, several baked goods are mentioned in the Hebrew Bible. Bread can be made in two ways, with a tray on an open fire (Lev 7:9; Isa 44:19)[17] and in a covered oven (Lev 26:26). Many archaeological excavations yielded remains of bread ovens (*ṭabbūn*) made of clay, while in several excavations fragments of bread trays were found.

DAIRY PRODUCTS. The meal served by Abraham to his guests (Gen 18:8) illustrates well that fresh milk was an important component of a sumptuous meal. Furthermore, fresh milk was also a thirst-quenching drink, as is depicted by the Jael and Sisera incident: "He [Sisera] said to her [Jael], 'Give me some water to drink, for I am thirsty.' She opened a skin of milk [and] gave him a drink" (Judg 4:19).[18]

Fresh milk cannot be stored for long without refrigeration, especially in the warm climate of the Near East. Therefore, to preserve it, milk has to be processed. The Mediterranean economy relied heavily on herding, and the herders learned to process the milk and turn it into several products, as hinted by the pre-Israelite story of Sinuhe, who was fed "milk in every (kind of) cooking."[19] This included yogurt, different kinds of butter, different kinds of cheese, and more.

Processing milk starts by churning, which separates the fat from the whey. This is done by using a container made of goatskin or clay. The vessel, still used in some present-day societies, is hung in a way that allows it to swing back and forth, a motion that separates the fat and permits the making of various products. Highly nutritious dairy products made and consumed by the Israelites were butter, cheese, and yogurt.

MEAT DISHES. Meat available for the Israelite kitchen included beef, veal, mutton, lamb, pork, fowl, and fish. The latter two are discussed separately below. Pork was prohibited for the Israelites but was consumed during certain periods by particular groups such as the Philistines, especially in the Iron Age I.[20] For the average Israelite, meat was not a daily fare. When served, meat was mostly of domesticated animals, although hunted animals were also available, as seen from certain biblical lists (Deut 14:5) and from zooarchaeological evidence. That hunted animals were considered a delicacy can be presumed from Isaac's request of Esau: "Take your hunting gear, your quiver and bow, and go out into the country and get me some game. Then make me a savory dish, the kind I like, and bring it for me to eat" (Gen 27:3–4). Game animals were sold to those who could not hunt or trap them, as evident from zooarchaeological data recovered in a market at Ashkelon. Domestic animals were available directly from the herd (Gen 18:7; 27:9; Judg 6:18–19) or were kept close to the house and fattened for special occasions (1 Sam 28:24).

There were several ways for preparing meat, and they were determined by the occasion. Extrabiblical sources and ethnographic studies indicate that for long storage meat was either smoked, dried, or salted. However, there is no mention in the Bible of such practices. Any biblical references to meat preparation relate to immediate consumption, usually on festive occasions such as hosting guests or during cultic festivals. One way of preparing meat was boiling it in water in a large pot.[21] A by-product of this process was broth, which was considered good enough to serve to honored guests (Judg 6:19–20). Another way of cooking meat was roasting it on an open fire. That this was not reserved just for festive occasions is suggested by references in Isa 44:16, 19, where the prophet mocks idol worshipers for using part of the same tree for carving idols and the rest for roasting meat.

Studies of culinary customs made in traditional Middle Eastern societies, such as bedouin and Druze communities, can demonstrate how meat was prepared and under what conditions.[22] The observation that "despite their varied geographical origins, Bedouin sacrificed sheep and goat in similar ways"[23] strongly suggests that these customs are old and might illustrate biblical modes of behavior. Bedouin families sacrifice at certain shrines, in a way reminiscent of what is described in 1 Sam 1:3. Furthermore, although the bedouin head of the family is the one to slit the animal's throat, others help in the butchering, and often a professional butcher (ashar), similarly to the tabbāh in 1 Sam 9:23–24, is entrusted with the dismembering.[24] The preferred sacrificial animal is a young male sheep or goat (6–12 months) and not older than 2.5 years, similar to certain biblical prescriptions.[25]

In traditional Middle Eastern societies, as it used to be in ancient times, meals with meat dishes signify special occasions, such as weddings and hosting guests, and are full of symbolism. Invitation, acceptance or refusal, and the protocol observed during the meal serve as means of communication. "The choice of meat served, the choice of dish served, and the order in which the guest(s) are served signal the recognition of social status, the importance of the occasion, and the seriousness of intent on the part of the host."[26] The host sits with the guests to encourage them to eat and see to all their needs, as with Abraham, who "there under the tree waited on them himself while they ate" (Gen 18:8). Nevertheless, no business should be discussed until, at the end of the meal, the host communicates his readiness.

Nowadays, the food is served on a large communal tray. During the Iron Age, large krater-bowls fulfilled this function. The order in which guests are served is representative of the social hierarchy perceived by the hosting society. While everyone eats from the communal tray, no one will take food from the tray or eat before the guest. Special parts are reserved for the guest. All these customs are well reflected in the way Samuel treated Saul on his visit:

> Samuel brought Saul and his servant into the dining-hall and gave them a place at the head of the invited company, about thirty in number. He said to the cook, "Bring the portion that I gave you and told you to put on one side." The cook took up the whole haunch and leg and put it before Saul, and Samuel said, "Here is the portion of meat kept for you. Eat it: it has been reserved for you at this feast to which I have invited the people." (1 Sam 9:22–24)

As demonstrated in this passage, certain parts of the animal, such as the breast and the right thigh, were considered choice and were reserved for the honored participants in the meal, who could be guests or priests. Other parts, such as the fat, kidneys, and liver, were always given to the priests.

SEAFOOD. Zooarchaeological and textual evidence indicate that the ancient Mediterranean diet included fish. We know that the Egyptians ate and exported fish and that the Israelites also ate fish. How often or how fish were prepared cannot be determined from present archaeological data. What can be determined is that not all the kinds of fish consumed at Israelite sites were in adherence to the biblical rule. Biblical instructions dictate that

> of creatures that live in water these may be eaten: all, whether in salt-water or fresh, that have fins and scales; but all, whether in salt or fresh water, that have neither fins nor scales, including both small creatures in shoals and larger creatures, you are to regard as prohibited.... Every

creature in the water that has neither fins nor scales is prohibited to you. (Lev 11:9–10, 12; see also Deut 14:9–10)

The Hebrew Bible refers to fish only in the collective *dāgâ*. No fish is mentioned by name, but zooarchaeological data from sites identified as Israelite show that the inhabitants of these settlements consumed a variety of fresh and saltwater fish. Remains of fresh and saltwater mollusks were discovered in smaller numbers at several sites, and it cannot be determined whether they were used as food or for other purposes such as jewelry and decoration. The small numbers of shells suggest that they were not the by-products of dyeing.

To be consumed, fresh fish can be boiled, fried, or roasted. Many inland sites have yielded fish remains, including bones and scales, and it is obvious that because of the distance from their source no fresh fish were consumed there. Although the Hebrew Bible does not mention anything concerning actual fish consumption or preparation, it does make references to fishing. Fishermen from Palestine as well as from other places such as Egypt supplied fish to inland settlements. Attesting to the lively market in fish is the fact that one of the gates in Jerusalem was named the Fish Gate (Zeph 1:10; Neh 3:3; 12:39; 2 Chr 33:14). To enable the transport of fish they first needed to be processed either by smoking or by drying and salting. Written and artistic extrabiblical sources illustrate that fish were processed before shipment. Egyptian sources demonstrate fish processing by first cleaning and then salting and drying them.[27]

FOWL. As with other living things, the Hebrew Bible contains prescriptions concerning the consumption of fowl. From the Iron Age and earlier, no architectural evidence is available showing that fowl were domesticated. Evidence, like columbaria (dove-cotes), is known from the later Hellenistic and Roman periods. However, the inclusion of certain birds in the sacrifice lists strongly suggests that pigeons and turtledoves were raised under controlled conditions. Bone remains of chickens, geese, and ducks from excavations at the Ophel in Jerusalem and other Iron Age sites show that these domestic types were available. Biblical references and zooarchaeological evidence demonstrate that certain wild birds were hunted. The consumption of birds was probably not different from what is practiced in the region today, which is similar to the consumption of other meats. Furthermore, like other animals, birds were fattened for consumption on special occasions, as suggested by the reference to *barbūrîm ʾăbûsîm,* "fattened fowl," that were served on Solomon's table (1 Kgs 5:3 [Eng. 4:23]).

Until the domestication of the chicken, eggs must have been available in limited quantities and thus were considered a delicacy. Two biblical references (Deut 22:6; Isa 10:14) suggest that eggs were available from the wild. That eggs were considered a delicacy is illustrated in Egyptian art, where images depict the offering of bowls filled with large eggs, possibly ostrich and pelican.[28]

FRUIT AND FRUIT PRODUCTS. While the valleys were suitable for field crops, the hill country was not as convenient for their cultivation. An efficient way of using the slopes was by building terraces and using the artificially created leveled plots for planting fruit trees of different kinds. Trees native to this region, which were planted and harvested, included figs, pomegranates, grape vines, apricots, date palms, apples, and olives. With the exception of the latter (see below), all these trees yield fruit that can be used in similar ways. In season, fruits of these trees can either be eaten fresh and their fresh juice drunk, or they can be processed for future use.

Other native fruit trees included the carob, which was probably very popular. The sweet-tasting pods are used today as chocolate substitute and might have been eaten in antiquity by those who had a sweet tooth. A poor person's fruit was the sycomore, which resembles a fig. This tree was quite common in Egypt, where the fruit was eaten and the wood was used for construction. Black mulberry and citron, a member of the citrus family, are also trees native to the region, but there are no references or any other evidence to the use of the fruit of these trees.[29]

Processing fruits for future consumption depends on the nature of each. Because of their high content of sugar, all the fruits mentioned above could be processed into alcoholic drinks. The most common for this purpose were grapes, followed by pomegranates. One other use for fruits was boiling them to make a thick, sweet syrup referred to in the Bible as dəbaš (honey). Grapes as well as figs, dates, and apricots can be dried, and the fruit can be preserved individually or put on a string or pressed into cakes. Dried fruit such as raisins were eaten as such when sweets were desired. Because of their high sugar content, they are the most efficient source of energy and were taken on long marches to provide energy. Trail mix has a long tradition.

DRINKS. The most common drinks for quenching thirst were water and milk; the latter was drunk sometimes in its processed form of yogurt (Judg 4:19; 5:25). A second drink made of a dairy by-product was whey. In season, fresh fruit juices were available. For long-term use, juices had to be preserved as alcoholic beverages, namely, wine. Grapes were the most common fruit to be made into wine, which could be used for secular purposes as well as on cultic occasions. Other fruits, such as pomegranates and dates, were also processed into wine.

Beer was another alcoholic beverage common in the ancient Near East. Since Egypt and Mesopotamia were well known as beer producers, it can be safely assumed that beer was also known in Israel, which is located between the two. Most scholars suggest that the biblical term *šēkār* refers to beer, while a few postulate that the reference is to grappa, a very strong distilled drink. Since there is no other term available for *beer,* one can conclude by process of elimination that biblical references to *šēkār* are quite possibly to beer. A different alcoholic beverage was mead (possibly *ṣûp,* Prov 16:24; Ps 19:11), which is made by mixing water and honey, then fermenting with malt, yeast, and other ingredients.

OTHER FOODS. The olive tree was considered one of the most important natural resources of Palestine because of its ability to provide oil (Deut 8:8). There were other oil-producing plants, such as sesame,[30] but olive oil was considered better tasting, more versatile, and had a longer "shelf life." Palestine was a major producer of olive oil not only for its inhabitants but also for other parts of the ancient Near East, such as Egypt and Mesopotamia. Olive oil can be used for a variety of purposes, such as lighting, cosmetics, medicine, and more. However, while one of its major uses is for food, written evidence does not provide us with much information in this respect. Remarkably little is said in the Bible concerning the use of oil in the kitchen. Although oil is used to a large extent in frying, this use is described mainly in relation to sacrifices, when recipes containing oil as an important component are listed: "one tenth of an *ʾēpâ*[31] of flour, the usual grain-offering, half of it in the morning and half in the evening. It is to be cooked with oil on a griddle. Bring it well-mixed and present it crumbled in small pieces as a grain-offering, a soothing odor to YHWH" (Lev 6:13–14 [Eng. 20–21]; see also 7:9–10, 12). While this recipe is for a "whole offering" and is not supposed to be eaten, it must reflect certain practices in the ancient Mediterranean kitchen.

Another food group that is not well known from the written and archaeological records is vegetables. The Bible talks little about vegetables, and when they are mentioned the attitude is mixed: at times they were considered a delicacy or even a must, and at times the lowliest food. Whatever was the attitude in some written documents, certain vegetables are native to this region and have been cultivated and eaten for millennia. These include carrots, cucumbers, musk and watermelons, onions, garlic, and more. Many leafy plants (field greens) and root plants were gathered in the wild and consumed as part of the meal. Dandelion greens are still picked by the locals for salads.

Other, mostly wild, plants used in the diet included nuts and berries. Among the nuts, we can include pistachios, walnut, pine nuts, and domesticated almonds. Among the berries native to this region, most prominent are the black mulberry and blackberry. A totally different food category is insects. According to Lev 11:20–23 certain grasshoppers were allowed to be eaten. They could be grilled on skewers or fried, and Assyrian reliefs demonstrate that these insects were considered a delicacy.

SPICES AND CONDIMENTS. Most foods do not taste good without seasoning. This can be done with either minerals, such as salt, or floral. The latter could be either cultivated or gathered in the wild. Some spices, whether minerals or floral, had to be imported. Salt, an important spice (Job 6:6), is a deposit found where saltwater evaporates; it originates in limited locations, so most communities had to purchase it. Its importance is demonstrated by the fact that it was also used as a sacrifice (Lev 2:13). Sources of salt were on the seacoast, whether the Mediterranean or the Dead Sea, and had to be transported to other parts.

Cultivated and wild-plant spices native to the region included cumin, black cumin, dill, coriander, thyme, black mustard, saffron, hyssop, mint, marjoram, fitches, capers, salt bush, dwarf chicory, reichardia, and more.[32] Imported plant spices included myrrh, galbanum, and cinnamon. Many plants were used for medicinal purposes and as perfumes and incense.

Although dried fruit were consumed as sweets, the most common sweetener was bee honey, from wild or domesticated bees. Other fruit-based sweeteners were thick syrups produced by boiling different kinds of fruit (e.g., dates) until the desired consistency was attained.

FOOD STORAGE

Food was eaten daily at home and on occasions in cultic sacrifices and offerings. Needless to say, not all food could be consumed immediately after production. Furthermore, it was in the interest of the producers to produce surplus so it could be used out of season and for trade and exchange. Storing of surplus depended on the nature of the product and the way it was meant to be used.

The most common item to be stored, which needed the largest space because of its volume, was grain. Storage of grain by the individual Israelite was done in pits and in jars. Stone-lined and plastered pits were located in various places in the compound, while storage in jars was done mostly in a storeroom in the house. The latter was a matter of convenience, providing close proximity of the grain to the grinding installations. Flour was also stored in jars, although the preference was to grind flour daily. On the basis of some of the Arad ostraca, one scholar calculated that the daily ration of bread was one loaf made out of one liter of flour. Under certain circumstances (e.g., military service), four days was the maximum for bread to remain edible. For a longer period, flour was issued.[33]

Jars of different sizes and shapes were used also for storage of liquids such as wine, oil, and water. Other items, such as dried fruit, were sometimes also stored in jars. Milk, however, was kept in a goatskin.

For long-time preservation, meat and milk had to be specially processed. Meat, as well as fish, could be preserved only by drying, salting, and/or smoking. Milk could be preserved for a long period as dry cheese.[34] The end products of these processes could be placed in baskets for future use.

Food Preparation and Consumption

Meals were eaten in the home, outside at work in the fields and orchards, in central cult places, and on the move while traveling or on military campaigns. The nature of the food consumed on these occasions depended on the place and the facilities available. It should be remembered that even when food consumption was outside the home, much of it was prepared ahead of time and was taken as ready-made.

The main installations directly involved in food preparation were for grinding grain and for baking and cooking.[35] Grinding grain, mostly of small quantities, was done in a mortar with pestle. The mortars were either portable or carved in bedrock. The end result of this activity was not flour but a rough mash or pulp that could be used for various dishes. Flour was produced with grinding stones, which were made of a pair of stones, upper and lower. The upper stone, which was smaller than the lower, was held in two hands and rubbed back and forth with the grain placed in between. Grinding installations were preferably made of hard stone such as basalt or flint. Grinding was a daily chore that provided fresh flour.

Dough was probably kneaded on a wooden board or trough placed on a stone workbench or on the floor. Baking was done in two ways: on a tray in an open fire (hearth) and in an oven. Baking ovens were round, dome-shaped installations constructed of clay. They were placed where the smoke would not hamper other activities, either in the courtyard or in a room by the door. Baking ovens were mostly individually owned by the household, but there were also shared ovens (Lev 26:26).[36] Fuel for ovens was mostly animal dung, and kindling fire was achieved by using small branches, straw, flax fibers, and olive-pressing leftovers.

Large bowls (kraters) made of clay or stone were used in food preparation for mixing of ingredients and as communal food-serving vessels. Certain dishes were cooked in a hearth in cooking pots of different shapes and sizes depending on what was cooked. Water was boiled in a pot shaped differently than the one used for cooking meat or for making gruel or stew. The latter were cooked in pots with a wide mouth so the food could be stirred and the pots could be covered with a flat stone or a large piece of pottery for better and faster results.

Although pans and griddles are not known in the ceramic repertoire of the Israelite period, certain biblical terms such as *marḥešet* suggest that there must have been such a utensil.

How many daily meals did the average Israelite eat? When were they eaten? What was served, and how was it consumed? Most of the cooked meals were eaten at home or at cult places. Cooked meals at home were eaten at the end of the workday. On special occasions, such as when guests arrived, they were eaten at the appropriate time. Field workers must have eaten something before leaving for work (Prov 31:15). At work, whether while herding or in the fields and orchards, food was mostly of the "take-out" variety. This was true also for travelers or for soldiers on maneuvers. These meals included bread, cheese and yogurt, vegetables in season, dried fruit, and water. During the appropriate season, field hands would eat parched grain and fresh fruit.

Cooked meals included mostly soup, gruel, and stew, which were served in individual bowls. The only utensil available was the knife, so eating was done by gulping and shoving food into the mouth and by grabbing the food by hand, probably with the help of a piece of flat bread. At the end of the meal, the dish or bowl was wiped clean with bread, as illustrated in the metaphor "I shall wipe Jerusalem as one wipes a plate and turns it upside down" (2 Kgs 21:13). Turning the dish upside down was probably a sign given by the eater that he or she had had enough.

While the average Israelites led their gastronomic lives basically as described above, the upper class (royalty, nobility, high priesthood) had a much richer diet, which must have affected their appearance and behavior (Deut 32:13–18). The prophet Amos rebukes the behavior of the upper class and their eating habits in Amos 6:4–6:

> You loll on beds inlaid with ivory and lounge on your couches;
> you feast on lambs from the flock and stall-fed calves;
> you improvise on the lute and like David invent musical instruments;
> you drink wine by the bowlful and anoint yourselves with the richest oils.

Health and Sickness

What do we know about the Israelites' physical and mental health? To learn about health and sickness in biblical times, we rely on written (biblical and extrabiblical) sources and on archaeological evidence, which is available from skeletal remains, from the analysis of the surrounding soil, and from the analysis of other remains (e.g., coprolites).

The vocabulary associated with this subject suggests that the Bible has a lot to offer in this respect, but the problem for the modern student is proper interpretation of the terms and lack of descriptive details of cases.

There are several general terms for disease and sickness (Deut 7:15; *ḥŏlî,* Deut 28:61; *negaʿ,* 1 Kgs 8:37; *dəway,* Ps 41:4, and *madweh,* Deut 7:15). Furthermore, there is a special term for plague (*maggēpâ*), which I will discuss later. Physical pain has its own terms. Two terms for strong pain, (*ṣîr* and *ḥebel*) are mostly reserved to depict childbirth contractions (Isa 13:8; 21:3). The more common term (*kəʾēb,* Isa 17:11) is used to describe pain in general. Physical injuries such as wounds have their own terminology.

The opposite of disease and sickness is the state of health and recovery. There are quite a few terms for wellness and recovery (*marpēʾ,* Mal 3:20; *rəpūʾôt,* Jer 30:13; 46:11; Ezek 30:21; and *ripʾût,* Prov 3:8) and for the healing process (*ʾărûkâ,* Jer 33:6; *māzôr,* Jer 30:13).

The Bible does not discuss mental sickness in detail; however, it acknowledges the existence of such a condition. The state of mental sickness is called *šiggāʿôn* (Deut 28:28; 2 Kgs 9:20; Zech 12:4). There are at least three detailed incidents describing situations with people suffering of mental imbalance. The first one describes Saul, who suffered of a "bad spirit" and was calmed down by David's music (1 Sam 16:14–23). The second occurs when David, escaping from Saul, appeared in Gath and for fear of the Philistine king Achish pretended to be crazy: "So he changed his behavior before them, and feigned himself mad in their hands, and made marks on the doors of the gate, and let his spittle run down his beard" (1 Sam 21:14 [Eng. 13]). The third incident pertains to the behavior of one of Elisha's followers who came to Jehu in Ramoth-gilead to anoint him as king over Israel (2 Kgs 9:1–12). No details are available, but there must have been something in his behavior to suggest that he was considered mentally imbalanced.

Physical handicaps (*mûm,* Lev 21:17–18) appear in the Bible mostly in a formulaic style. Lists of handicaps prescribe who was not fit to serve as priest. These lists are reinforced by similar ones describing animals not fit for sacrifice (Lev 22:19–25). The most commonly mentioned handicap is blindness (*ʿiwwārôn,* Deut 28:28; Zech 12:4).[37] The second most mentioned handicap is lameness.[38] From the story of David's capture of Jerusalem, it seems that people suffering from these handicaps were kept at the edge of or outside the city (2 Sam 5:6–8). One particular individual who is known to have been "lame as to both his feet" was Mephibosheth, son of Saul (2 Sam 9:13; 19:27). According to 2 Sam 4:4, his condition was the result of childhood injury. Other handicaps that are mentioned in several of the biblical texts are deafness (*ḥērēš,* Lev 19:14) and dumbness (*ʾillēm,* Exod 4:11).

Other handicaps listed in Lev 21:18, 20 and Deut 28:27 include being humpbacked and thin. Other terms on the list, which are not fully understood, possibly include defective sight, enlarged testicle, mutilated, too long of limb, having a scab or scar, scurf, and having an itch or rash. The last three terms can be viewed as diseases rather than handicaps because of the way in which they appear in other contexts.

Most named diseases mentioned in the Bible are skin diseases. For example, Deut 15:2–15 deals with a situation of skin discharge, possibly pus. Strict instructions are given not to touch the sick person or any object touched by him. The cure for the afflicted was achieved by washing with water, while anything and anyone touched by him was also to be washed. On the eighth day after he was cured, he was to make a sacrifice.

Likewise, Lev 13 is a treatise on a particular skin disease. After the text provides a list of symptoms, it defines the affliction as ṣārāʿat, usually translated "leprosy." However, according to the description of the symptoms, this disease is not modern leprosy, that is, Hansen's disease. Several types of the biblical disease are extant, some of which pertain to inanimate objects and possibly can be understood as mold or mildew. Objects afflicted by the so-called leprosy were to be burned. One strain of the disease afflicted people. The treatment states that the afflicted was to be quarantined and examined for a certain period every seven days. Only after certain physical signs proved that the person was healthy could he or she be released to society. From all the descriptions of this disease, it appears that it was or was believed to be a communicable disease and came as a punishment from YHWH.

Three individuals are singled out as ones who were afflicted by the so-called leprosy. Miriam, Moses' sister, became sick after chastising Moses for marrying a black woman (Num 12); Naaman, commander of the king of Aram's army (2 Kgs 5), was cured of his disease by bathing in the Jordan River seven times; and Uzziah, king of Judah, was placed in Beth ha-Hophshith and was never cured (2 Kgs 15:5; 2 Chr 26:19).

Another skin disease, this one causing sores (ʾăbaʿbūʿōt, Exod 9:9–10), was boils (šəḥîn). It could afflict humans as well as animals. King Hezekiah was cured by having a cake of dried figs rubbed on his sores (2 Kgs 20:7; Isa 38:2–7). Another person who was afflicted with this disease and later cured was Job (Job 2:7).

Internal diseases mentioned in the Bible are not better understood than are skin diseases. In Deut 28:22, a list of internal diseases possibly includes consumption of the lungs (šaḥepet), high fever (qaddaḥat), inflammation (dalleqet), fever (ḥarḥur), and pestilence (ḥereb = sword). There are two additional diseases on this list that can be identified, with the help of Jer 30:6, as jaundice or anemia (yērāqôn) and thinness or anorexia (šiddāpôn). This interpretation is on the basis of context and by linguistic and etymological analyses. Another malady, ṭəḥōrîm (Deut 28:27; 1 Sam 5:6–12), is identified as hemorrhoids. The Philistines were afflicted by this disease after capturing the ark of the covenant and were cured only upon returning the ark.

A few individuals are described as being sick, among them Jehoram, king of Judah, who died of an intestinal disease, possibly dysentery or acute diarrhea. "Yhwh smote him in his bowels with an incurable disease. In the course of time, at the end of two years, his bowels came out because of the disease, and he died in great agony" (2 Chr 21:18–19). Other individuals who are mentioned in the Bible as having been sick are the son of the widow whom Elijah revived (1 Kgs 17:17–24);[39] Elisha the prophet, who was mortally sick (2 Kgs 13:14); Ahaziah, king of Israel, who fell and got injured or sick (2 Kgs 1:2); and Joash, king of Judah, who while being ill with an undisclosed malady was assassinated by his servants (2 Chr 24:25).

The worst disease that could possibly affect human and animal populations was pestilence (*deber*). Several times pestilence is equated with sword (*ḥereb*, Lev 26:25), and at times the word *sword* replaces *pestilence*. Furthermore, at numerous times these two appear together with famine (*rāʿāb*). Yhwh used all three devastating forces to bring total destruction. The infliction of pestilence is many times referred to as plague (*maggēpâ*), and it came as Yhwh's punishment for misconduct. Sometimes Yhwh inflicted the plague by sending a messenger (*malʾāk*) with a sword (1 Chr 21:15, 27); thus it can be safely assumed that when the *malʾāk* of Yhwh appeared overnight in the Assyrian camp at Jerusalem, it was pestilence (2 Kgs 19:35). Some of the more famous incidents of pestilence mentioned in the Bible occurred during the wandering in the desert (Num 14:37; 17:13–15; 25:8–18). Another one struck the Israelites after David conducted a census (2 Sam 24:13–17; 1 Chr 17).

According to Israelite understanding, the sources for sickness were two: (1) ideological, namely, Yhwh's response to misbehavior such as breaking the covenant; and (2) physical, namely, close association with a sick person that led to contagion and contamination. The first factor was dealt with by prayer, observing the covenant, and by sacrifice; the second was dealt with by quarantine and ritual purification.

There are no biblical references to any type of surgery except to circumcision, which at times is described as being performed with flint blades (Exod 4:25; Josh 5:3–4). There is archaeological evidence for some surgical procedures such as trephination (also known as craniotomy), the removal of a portion of bone from the cranium without penetrating the underlying soft tissue. This delicate procedure is known from the Neolithic and Chalcolithic periods in Jericho and environs, and there is some evidence from Lachish that it was also practiced in the Iron Age.[40] The procedure was known and documented also during the Roman period. Judging from biblical references, the Israelites' knowledge of anatomy was limited and probably came mostly from the slaughtering and butchering of animals. Internal parts mentioned are heart, kidneys, and liver, which are all perceived as loci of emotions and intelligence.

Hygiene and Sanitation

Good health, quality of life, and longevity depend heavily on two factors: good hygiene and proper sanitation. The discussion of the topic of hygiene relies heavily on the biblical record and its interpretation, which sometimes relies on ethnographic information. Supporting archaeological evidence is meager and cannot contribute much to the understanding of this topic.[41]

Personal Hygiene

The limited availability of water made cleanliness a constant problem. Daily washing was probably limited to hands and faces. The importance of clean hands became a metaphor for a clean conscience (Deut 21:6; 2 Sam 22:21; Ps 18:21, 25; Job 9:30; 22:30). Washing of the feet became part of the hospitality ritual (Gen 18:4; 19:2; 24:32; 43:24; Judg 19:21; 1 Sam 25:41). Biblical references strongly suggest that washing of the feet was done in a large bowl or pot (*sîr,* Pss 60:10; 108:10).[42] The priests were required to wash their hands and feet in basins before performing their duties (Exod 30:18–19, 21; 40:30–31; Deut 21:6; 2 Chr 4:6).

Average individuals probably did not have a chance to have a full-body bath very often unless they lived by a source of running water such as a brook. Sometimes washing in certain bodies of water, as in the case of Naaman the Aramean washing in the Jordan (2 Kgs 5), was considered purifying and remedial. Women probably washed more often than men, most likely as part of flirting (Song 5:3; Ruth 3:3) and purifying after menstruation. Bathsheba, the wife of Uriah the Hittite, was taking a full-body bath, possibly in her courtyard, when David, who was on the roof of his house, saw her and liked her (2 Sam 11:2).

Whether people used soap when washing can be only guessed. Both the expression "clean hands" and the biblical term for soap stem from the same verb root, *brr.* Jeremiah 2:22 proclaims: " 'Though you wash [*kbs*] with lye [*neter*] and use much soap [*bōrît*], the stain of your sin is still before me,' says the Lord Y_HWH_." The verb used here for washing is usually used in the context of washing clothes, but it can be interpreted also as for washing the body. Soap (*bōrît,* Mal 3:2) was used in doing laundry. It was potash soap, which is a soft soap made from the lye leached from wood ashes. Several biblical references mention the washing of clothes (*kbs*). How often people washed their clothes cannot be determined; however, limited water sources made the performance of this activity an infrequent affair. It seems that having laundry done on a regular basis was reserved for the rich (2 Sam 19:25), a task that was probably carried out by professionals who gave the name of their profession to the area where they practiced their chore (Isa 7:3; 36:2 = 2 Kgs 18:17).

The Bible mentions the ritual washing of the body and clothes. When the blood of a sacrifice splattered on a piece of clothing, it needed to be washed (Lev 6:20). Whoever touched the carcass of a clean or an unclean animal was to wash his clothes (Lev 11:25, 28, 40). When people were afflicted with a skin disease, part of the recovery process demanded the washing of their clothes (Lev 13:6, 34; 14:8–9). A similar treatment is prescribed for a man who suffered from "a discharge from his member," had "an emission of semen," or touched a menstruating woman (Lev 15). A piece of clothing that was showing signs of mildew was to be washed (Lev 13:54–55, 58). While washing clothes seems to have been an integral part of purity (Exod 19:10, 14), there is no way to find out how closely these prescriptions were observed and who could have enforced them.

To overcome body odor, people—mostly women—used perfumes. Perfumes were used to mask the foul odor also in burial caves where multiple burials took place, as can be seen from the numerous black perfume juglets that were excavated in many of the Iron Age II caves. To counteract odors in public places and in the homes, incense and spices were used. Some were manufactured locally, while some were imported from distant lands.[43]

SANITATION

Sanitation and general cleanliness are highly important in determining healthy living conditions. As with hygiene, the information available about this topic as it relates to the Israelite period—whether written or archaeological—is scant and needs careful interpretation. There is no evidence that any of the cities and villages in the period and area under discussion had any systems for the disposal of sewage. Any channels that were recovered in archaeological excavations belonged to systems for collection of runoff rainwater. Rainwater was collected from roofs and streets and diverted into water cisterns for later use. Some cisterns were privately owned, and some were part of a central system.

Disposal of garbage was done by sweeping the house floors and cleaning the refuse directly into the street or by throwing it over the city wall. On the one hand, these habits created middens outside the city; on the other, they raised the level of the street. As a result of this process, after a period occupants had to go down into their houses. Furthermore, garbage in the street (*repeš ḥûṣôt* or *ṭîṭ ḥûṣôt,* 2 Sam 22:43; Isa 57:20; Mic 7:10; Zech 9:3; 10:5; Ps 18:43) contaminated the water systems that relied on collection of runoff water. This, in turn, contributed to the spread of disease and the ill health of the inhabitants.

An acute problem in Israelite towns and villages was the disposal of human excrements. The biblical instruction is simple: "You shall have a designated area outside the camp to which you shall go. With your equipment you shall have a trowel [*yātēd*]; when you squat outside, you shall dig a hole with it and then cover up your excrement [*ṣē'ātekā*]" (Deut 23:13–14 [Eng. 12–13]). This might explain the dearth of evidence. Unlike from the Roman period, few sanitary facilities from the Iron Age in Palestine have been discovered in archaeological excavations. Two latrines were uncovered in Jerusalem during recent excavations. Two other stone seats were discovered in Jerusalem in earlier excavations. One of the latrines was excavated in a well-to-do house in the City of David, and the contents of the cesspit were analyzed.[44] The analysis showed that lime was used in an attempt to sanitize the latrine by reducing bacterial and fungal activity. In addition to the pollen of the consumed food, the fecal matter contained eggs from two human intestinal parasites, tapeworm (*taenia*) and whipworm (*trichuris trichiura*). The former can be the result of consumption of poorly cooked, maybe even raw, beef or pork. The latter indicates "an infection arising either from the ingestion of fecally contaminated foods or from unsanitary living arrangements in which people came into contact with human excrement."[45] This could have happened if the sanitary conditions were poor or the food consumed was grown in gardens fertilized with human waste and was unwashed. Since the final use of the latrines was during the Babylonian siege of Jerusalem, it is possible that the analysis reflects extraordinary conditions. Similar conditions are described in Ezek 4:12, where bread is said to have been baked with human dung as fuel.

However, it seems that poor sanitary and food-preservation conditions were not only the results of siege. Under normal circumstances people, including the rich, suffered from intestinal diseases and parasites: "YHWH struck him [King Jehoram] in his bowels with an incurable disease. In the course of time, at the end of two years, his bowels came out because of the disease, and he died in great agony" (2 Chr 21:18–19).

The expression *maštîn baqqîr*, meaning "he who urinates at the wall," which is always used in announcing the future extinction of all males in the family, is a reflection of the manner by which males relieved themselves. This could have been done outside the house in a corner and must have contributed to the poor sanitary conditions described above.

LIFE CYCLES

Life in ancient Israel ran in cycles and revolved around certain events, secular and cultic. The events, mostly related to the economy, were closely tied with nature, hence their cyclical character. Since the cultic events were discussed above (chs. 2 and 3), I would like to deal here with some of the events that marked certain stages in the life of the individual. The discussion below will touch on some points in life common to the urban and rural societies, such as birth, marriage, death, and the laws and customs by which they were governed and celebrated.

I cannot overemphasize the fact that the background of Israelite society was rural, whether agrarian or pastoral, and its laws and customs were formulated and formed against this background. So, whenever we discuss such matters we should not forget their place of origin and the reasons that might have prompted their genesis. Life cycles were closely related to the rural background and should be viewed as such.[46]

BIRTH

Birth and marriage are related through sexual activity, so this will be the first topic discussed.[47] From the biblical viewpoint, the main purpose of sexual activity was procreation, which was supposed to provide offspring who would participate in the necessary economic chores and produce heirs to inherit and maintain the family possessions. Therefore, a family with many children was the ultimate blessing (Ps 128:3). Procreation was the linchpin of many biblical blessings (Gen 9:1, 7; 12:2; 15:18; 26:3–4). This does not preclude the notion that there was sexual desire (Gen 3:16)[48] and that sometimes it led to objectionable behavior such as adultery, incest, rape, bestiality, and homosexuality. To provide an outlet for sexual desire that could not be fulfilled within the prescribed norms, Israelite society tolerated secular prostitution.[49]

The Israelites considered children to be a blessing, and barrenness was compared to being dead (Gen 30:1). The birth of a child was celebrated by the giving of a meaningful name, an act that was carried out by the father (Gen 21:3; 25:26) or the mother (Gen 30:6, 8, 11, 13, 18, 20, 21, 24). Another act of initiating the baby into Israelite society was the circumcision of all male children (Gen 21:4). The Bible reports that this was done with flint knives (Exod 4:25; Josh 5:2–3). Circumcision was recognized as the mark of being a member of the YHWH-worshiping Israelite community.

MARRIAGE

Ensuring that its possessions remained in family hands was the force behind having children and the formulation of certain laws, especially those concerned with inheritance. Thus Deut 21:15–17 states clearly that only sons could inherit and that the first son was to receive "a double share of all that he [the father] possesses." That this was the custom is illustrated by several narratives, such as those about Ishmael and Isaac (Gen 21:10) and Isaac and his half-brothers (Gen 25:5–6). The stories describing the blessings given to Jacob instead of Esau (Gen 27) and to Ephraim in place of Manasseh (Gen 48:13–20) come to demonstrate the same attitude. Women inherited only under special circumstances. That they had some rights when there were no male heirs is pointed out through the claim of

Leah and Rachel for their share (Gen 31:14–16). A case in point is that of the daughters of Zelophehad, which must have been a real legal precedent because it is mentioned more than once and in different circumstances (Num 26:33; 27:1–11; 36:2–12; Josh 17:3–6; 1 Chr 7:15). Since the family did not have a male heir, the five daughters (Mahlah, Noah, Hoglah, Milcah, Tirzah) were given a special dispensation to inherit their father's *naḥălâ*, but with one provision, that they would not marry outside the tribe. This was done to assure that the land would never be lost to the clan. That this was a long-standing custom can be surmised by the story of Job's three beautiful daughters, who received "an inheritance with their brothers" (Job 42:15). The Samaria ostraca (see ch. 6), which contain the names of two of Zelophehad's daughters (Noah and Hoglah), strongly suggest that the biblical references have a foundation in real life.[50]

Marriage was one way of protecting the family inheritance; this was done by arrangement between the families.[51] That marriage was a socioeconomic and political tool is well illustrated by the arranged marriages between different royal houses to secure their future relationships. The favored arranged marriage among the common Israelites was within the clan, especially between cousins (Gen 24; 28:1–9). Because of low life expectancy for women and the risk of barrenness, it was common to take more than one wife. Furthermore, a barren wife could give her husband a surrogate wife, as in the case of the maidservants of Sarah, Leah, and Rachel. When the husband died with no male heirs, levirate marriage was practiced, as described in detail in the book of Ruth (see also Gen 38; Deut 25:5–10).

The Bible does not mention a particular age for women to be married, and for men it is vague.[52] Neither is mention made of any particular ceremony that took place.[53] However, since a dowry (*šillūḥîm*) was given to the bride by the bride's father (Gen 29:24, 29; 1 Kgs 9:16) and presents (*mōhar*) were given by the groom to the bride and to her father (Gen 24:53; 34:12; Exod 22:15–16 [Eng. 16–17]; 1 Sam 18:25), the exchange can be considered a business transaction. This is probably the reason why divorce had to be carried out in writing by giving the wife "divorce papers" (*sēper kərîtût,* Deut 24:1–4; Isa 50:1; Jer 3:8). Israelite society recognized second marriages as a result of divorce or widowhood, but a woman being married for the first time was expected to be a virgin (Deut 22:13–21). Pre- and extramarital sex, especially adultery, were forbidden and punishable by death (Deut 22:22–26).

Not all marriages followed the norm. Some marriages were carried out by force, such as that of Dinah, daughter of Jacob (Gen 34) and that of the women of Shiloh (Judg 21:19–23; also Deut 22:28–29). Some were mixed marriages, as exemplified by that of Esau (Gen 26:34; 36:2) and Joseph (Gen 41:45). Other marriages did not follow the regular formula, such as

Samson's first marriage, where he, the groom, was involved in the negotiations (Judg 14).

DEATH AND BURIAL

Death is the physical and spiritual end of the individual.[54] When discussing death from the Israelite point of view, we need to look at their attitude toward this phenomenon and the way it was handled, namely, the disposition of the body.

Death was unavoidable (Gen 3:19) and could come in several ways, peaceful as well as violent. The preference, of course, was to have a peaceful death at an old age with a large family to carry on the family traditions (Gen 25:7–9; 46:30). All dead resided in Sheol (Heb. *šə'ôl*),[55] the Israelite understanding of which changed with time. Generally it was considered a pit (Isa 14:15) located deep in the earth (Ezek 31:15). Some scholars suggest that certain biblical references identify the grave with Sheol. Sheol had gates (Isa 38:10), a feature probably influenced by Egyptian and Mesopotamian views of the underworld. The residents of Sheol were sometimes called *rəpā'îm*, the etymology of which is not very clear. Those who went down to Sheol were not able to return, but consulting the dead (necromancy), though forbidden in Israel (Deut 18:11; cf. 1 Sam 28:3), was practiced to a certain extent (1 Sam 28).

The deceased was buried as soon as possible before sundown, a courtesy extended even to criminals and enemies (Deut 21:22–23; Josh 10:26–27). Cremation was practiced only under very special circumstances (1 Sam 31:12).

Burial took place in a variety of locations, though archaeologically only a certain type of burials from the Israelite period has been excavated. According to biblical traditions, when people died during transition from one location to another they were buried by the road, as for example happened to Rachel (Gen 35:19–20; 1 Sam 10:2), Miriam (Num 20:1), Aaron (Num 33:39; Deut 10:6), and Moses (Deut 34:6). If there were a distinguished marker such as a tree, the deceased was buried there, as for example happened to Deborah, Rebecca's nurse (Gen 35:8), and to Saul and his sons (1 Sam 31:12–13). Being buried by a tree might have a connection with the "tree of life." Biblical traditions assign a cave, the Cave of Machpelah, as a burial place for the patriarchs and the matriarchs (except for Rachel). Others were buried in the family plot, such as Gideon (Judg 8:32), Samson (Judg 16:31), and Asahel (2 Sam 2:32). Some were buried on their land (*naḥălâ*) or on its boundary, such as Joshua (Josh 24:30), Joseph (Josh 24:32), and Eleazar (Josh 24:33). This custom assured the claim to the land.[56] Embalming was not practiced by the Israelites, and only Jacob and Joseph are described as being embalmed because, according to tradition, they died in Egypt.

During the Late Bronze Age, on the verge of the Israelite appearance in Canaan, burials took place in burial caves, pits, or cist and bench tombs. Some burials took place in ceramic coffins, jars, and anthropoid coffins. During the Israelite period, the burial form became standardized, and those who could afford it chose to be buried in a family burial cave that was located in a cemetery outside the town's limits. Only the kings of Israel and Judah were buried inside the capital city. Some archaeologists identify a set of manmade caves in the City of David with the royal burial grounds of the house of David. Others suggest that a series of burial caves located on the grounds of St. Etienne monastery north of the Old City of Jerusalem are royal tombs.

The common Israelite burial cave during the Iron Age was entered through a small, rectangular entrance that could be blocked with one large, flat stone. Two to three steps led into the burial chamber, where one to three benches lined the walls. A suggestion has been made that the tomb plan mirrors the plan of the four-room house. The body of the deceased was placed on one of the benches, which sometimes had a depression for the head and a raised lip along the edge of the bench. A few benches in tombs in Jerusalem had raised headrests shaped like a horseshoe. Some tombs had niches in the walls or depressions in the benches for the placement of oil lamps. Special pits—repositories—carved in the room corners across from the entrance or under the benches were used for the collection of bones and other funerary objects. These include clay vessels, figurine, jewelry, weaponry, and such.

This tomb type was for multiple burials and was used as a family burial plot. Even when all benches were occupied, they were reused whenever a new burial had to take place. The remains from a previous burial (bones, objects) were placed in the repository, and a new burial was performed on the cleared bench. This explains the expression so often used in the Bible: "he slept/was laid with his fathers."

Some of the tombs belonging to well-to-do families were large, contained more than one chamber, and had carved decorations and grave markers. Some burials had inscriptions outside or inside the tomb warning against break-ins or asking the deity for a blessing. Some biblical references suggest that a sacrifice was made and that ancestor worship was practiced to a certain degree. This custom is associated with the term *marzēaḥ* employed by Jeremiah (16:5) and Amos (6:7). One burial custom referred to many times is the lamenting over the dead that was carried out not only by the family members but also by professional mourners.

Many Iron Age bench tombs can be found throughout Palestine, and large numbers of them surround Jerusalem. The use of this tomb type continued for many centuries and was practiced with a few modifications as late as the Roman period.

For Further Study:

Bloch-Smith, Elizabeth. *Judahite Burial Practices and Beliefs about the Dead.* Journal for the Study of the Old Testament Supplement Series 123. Sheffield: JSOT Press, 1992.
   The most comprehensive study on the subject of death and burials in Judah during the Israelite period. The work deals not only with the actual burial practices and customs but also with the Judahite theology of death and afterlife.
Brothwell, Don R., and Patricia Brothwell. *Food in Antiquity: A Survey of the Diet of Early People.* New York: Praeger, 1969.
   Although somewhat outdated, this work is still worth consulting when dealing with food in antiquity. It provides a wealth of information on all food groups, food preparation, and nutrition.
Frankel, Rafael, Shmuel Avitsur, and Etan Ayalon. *History and Technology of Olive Oil in the Holy Land.* Translated by Jay C. Jacobson. Arlington, Va., Oléarius Editions; Tel Aviv: Eretz Israel Museum, 1994.
   Since olive oil was an important commodity in biblical (and other) times, the way it was produced is highly important. This work by three experts describes oil production through the ages, with excellent illustration of installations and implements.
Neufeld, Edward. "Hygiene Conditions in Ancient Israel (Iron Age)." *Biblical Archaeologies* 34 (1971): 42–66.
   Not much has been written on this topic, so this article is highly important because it covers many aspects of the topic, relying on biblical, extrabiblical, and archaeological sources. Some of the issues discussed are drainage and sewage disposal, sanitation, personal hygiene, cleanliness during cooking, and more.

5

ANCIENT ISRAELITE ARTS

When discussing art as part of Israelite culture, I approach the topic with the modern attitude that this includes both visual and performing art. Thus, under this heading I discuss music, dance, painting, sculpting, carving, and other modes of art.

Like the surrounding cultures, Israelite culture included some refined elements such as visual and performing arts. As with other facets of daily life, these, too, were influenced to a certain degree by the surrounding cultures. Unfortunately, when it comes to visual arts, not much is preserved due to the nature of the materials used. As for ancient music and dance, the situation is much worse because all that survived are limited verbal descriptions, a few artistic representations, and several physical remains of musical instruments. Most of our knowledge, then, depends mainly on interpretation of this evidence, and on educated guesswork based on ethnographic studies of present-day societies and comparisons with the neighboring ancient cultures of Egypt and Mesopotamia.

PERFORMING ARTS: MUSIC AND DANCE

Numerous biblical references to music and dance show that both were an integral part of Israelite life. As in modern times, music in biblical times was both vocal and instrumental, and it was part of a long tradition in the ancient Near East. From written records and artistic representations it appears that most of the times dance was accompanied by music.[1]

The Bible attributes the invention of instrumental music to Jubal, who "was the ancestor of those who play the lyre [*kinnôr*] and lute [*'ûgāb*]" (Gen 4:21).[2] Music was played both in private and on public occasions, secular as well as cultic. Similarly, dance was performed on a variety of occasions, as can be seen in wall paintings and stone reliefs. Many of the public musical performances were carried out by professionals, as suggested by the guild names mentioned in the Psalms and in other biblical references. The names of the eponymous founders of the guilds—Asaph, Heman, and Jeduthun—first appear in the description of David's preparations for the construction of the temple (1 Chr 25:1–7), then in the description of the inauguration of Solomon's temple (2 Chr 5:12) and later in the Passover celebration by Josiah (2 Chr 35:15). The professional status of singers and dancers must have been enhanced during the time of the monarchy. This is well illustrated in the list of booty taken by Sennacherib from Hezekiah, which included "male and female musicians."[3]

BIBLICAL MUSIC AND MUSICAL INSTRUMENTS[4]

Several musical instruments are mentioned throughout the Hebrew Bible. One reference containing the names of five instruments, all in Aramaic, appears in the book of Daniel in a description of a cultic event: "When you hear the sound of horn [*qarnāʾ*], pipe [*mašrôqîtāʾ*], zither [*qatros*],[5] triangle [*sabkāʾ*], dulcimer [*pəsantərîn*], a full consort of music [*sûmpônyâ*], ... prostrate yourselves and worship the gold image that King Nebuchadnezzar has set up" (Dan 3:5; also 7, 10, 15). Although this description is included in one of the late books of the Bible, it is not different from what is known from earlier sources. A clay representation from Palestine of a musical group is depicted on the musician stand from Ashdod (see fig. 5.1).[6] This Philistine fenestrated incense stand shows four individuals each using a different musical instrument. The instruments on the stand and in the references in the book of Daniel represent some of the groups to which biblical instruments belonged, including percussion, membrane, wind, and string instruments.

1. Percussion instruments are made of reverberating materials that give off sounds when shaken or struck. This group contains instruments such as rattles (*mənaʿănʿîm*), small and large cymbals (*məṣiltayim*), sistrums (*ṣelṣelîm* or *šālîš*), and bells (*paʿămôn*). A variety of these instruments, including cymbals, sistrums, bells, rattles, and clappers, have been discovered in several archaeological excavations. In Palestine, a sistrum was

Fig. 5.1. Musician stand, Ashdod. Courtesy Israel Antiquities Authority.

discovered at Tel Miqne-Ekron and a pair of bronze cymbals dating roughly 1200–1000 B.C.E. at Megiddo. Some of the rattles in ancient Israel were made of clay and contained one or more pellets that made noise when shaken.

2. Membrane instruments produce sound by striking a membrane (often skin) stretched over a frame, such as a drum or tambourine (*tôp*). The nature of these instruments does not lend itself to good preservation. In Palestine, clay figurines of a female tambourine player demonstrating how the instrument was used have survived from Taanach and Shiqmona (see fig. 5.2).

3. Wind instruments produce sound due to the passage of air in, through, or around them. This category includes (a) the double (v-shaped) pipe, single pipe (*ḥālîl*), or lamentation-pipe (*nəḥîlôt*);[7] and (b) trumpet (*ḥăṣōṣərâ*) or horn (*šôpār, qeren,* and *yôbēl*). Archaeological finds and written evidence indicate that different

Fig. 5.2. Female tambourine player. Courtesy Israel Antiquities Authority.

materials such as bone, wood, reed, and silver were used to make the different kinds of pipes. Tutankhamun's tomb yielded two trumpets made of copper or bronze with gold overlay.[8] Other excavations yielded true end-blown flutes and double reed-pipes of both the clarinet and oboe types.[9] Wind instruments were played standing as well as in the seated position. A bronze figurine from Byblos dated to the second millennium B.C.E. illustrates the seated stance of a flute player.[10] The musician stand from Ashdod[11] as well as paintings from Egypt and stone reliefs from Mesopotamia illustrate the standing stance.

4. String instruments produce sound by plucking or bowing of strings extended over a sounding box. These include lyre (*kinnôr*), large *kinnôr* (*nēbel*), and lute.[12] A recent study of the geographical and temporal spread of the term *kinnôr* and its cognates suggests that the biblical references relate to a lyre of the Eastern (thin flat-based) type with four to eight strings that usually required a plectrum.[13] A depiction of such a lyre, probably Canaanite, comes from Megiddo Stratum VIIA.[14] The term *nebel* refers to the thick lyre with ten to thirteen strings, which did not require

a plectrum.[15] A clay figurine from Ashdod depicts a musician playing this lyre-type instrument.[16] A bronze figurine from Beth-shean dated to the twelfth century B.C.E., showing a standing woman wearing a wreath-type headdress playing a long-necked lute, illustrates playing the lute.[17] A similar pose can be seen in an Eighteenth Dynasty tomb painting[18] that portrays a lute player, a harp player, and possibly singers and/or dancers.

MUSICAL NOTES

How did biblical music sound? Although we have some vague idea of how Israelite music would have sounded, presently there is no way to re-create it. However, some musical terms, found mostly in the Psalms, survived and might lend themselves in the future to musical reconstruction. Some psalms contain instructions to the music leader (*mənaṣṣēaḥ*), definition of the composition (*mizmôr, maśkîl, təhillâ, təpillâ,* and *šîr*), musical instructions, and references to the performing guild. All these make us realize that music was a well-developed performance art.

MUSICAL PERFORMANCE

Music was performed for a variety of reasons and on multiple occasions. Performances were carried out in private or public, for religious as well as secular reasons. There are many ways to define the nature and occasion for musical performances. However, at times it is hard clearly to define whether the occasion was secular or religious. Performances were vocal, instrumental, or both and were done by professionals or lay people. Many times they accompanied dance (Job 21:11–12), which was either organized or spontaneous. Following is an attempt to describe some of these occurrences and their nature.

PRIVATE PERFORMANCE

Private performances can be considered generally secular and non-professional, mostly spontaneous, but at various times they were organized. They took place when people were engaged in daily, mundane chores indoors and out. At home, mothers sang to their children to calm them or during the execution of routine work such as grinding flour, preparing food, and weaving. Much of the musical performances that can be defined as private took place during outdoors activities such as watching over the herds, working in the fields and gardens, or during processing agricultural produce in the wine and olive presses (treading grapes, Jer 25:30; 48:32–33) and at the threshing floor. Other times in which singing was done occurred while carrying out monotonous chores such as digging a well (Num 21:16–18) or shearing sheep (2 Sam 14:28).

When someone suffered from a bad mood, he or she could get some relief by having someone play a musical instrument such as the lyre, as in the case of David playing for Saul (1 Sam 16:16–23). Music playing and singing were performed during drinking bouts (Amos 6:4–5) and at outdoor dancing (Song 7:1 [Eng. 6:13]) in the vineyards (Judg 21:19–21).

Music and singing were carried out on private occasions in a limited number of religious performances, such as worship in the home shrine, during burials, and while mourning. Praising was also sometimes a private affair, as in Hannah's song after the birth of Samuel (1 Sam 2:1–10).

PUBLIC PERFORMANCE

Musical public performances were mostly organized and carried out by professionals, although at times it was a spontaneous outburst by nonprofessionals. Professional musicians engaged in public performance are known to have existed throughout the ancient Near East, as for example in Mesopotamia. Their activities are well documented and known from cuneiform tablets. Egyptian tomb paintings illustrate the variety of instruments played by professional court musicians and the activities of professional dancers.[19] The Ashdod musician stand represents elements in the Philistine cult that involved public performance. This was not different from Israelite public performance, because the stand depicts cult functionaries like the ones mentioned in 2 Chr 5:12–13, which included Levitical singers and musicians belonging to professional guilds. The scenes on the stand are also reminiscent of what is described in 1 Sam 10:5, when Saul met "a company of prophets coming down from the shrine, led by a *nēbel* [large *kinnôr*], *tōp* [drum], *ḥālîl* [fife], and *kinnôr* [lyre], and filled with prophetic rapture."

SECULAR OCCURRENCES. First and foremost among secular musical performances were events related to military activities, which provided opportunities for the use of music in different venues. Certain wind instruments, especially the *šôpār,* were used for summoning and signaling (Judg 3:27; 6:34). The ram's horn was also used to stun the enemy (Josh 6:3–16; Judg 7:15–21). When the battle was over, music (often accompanied by dancing) was used for victory celebration, such as after the crossing of the Sea of Reeds, the victory over Sisera by Deborah and Barak, and other occasions (Exod 15:1–18, 20–21; Num 21:27–30; Judg 5; 11:34; 1 Sam 18:6–7; 2 Sam 22). Since the outcome was not always favorable, music was also used to accompany laments over the fallen heroes, as after the fall of Saul and Jonathan (2 Sam 1:17–27). Some of the songs that were composed to celebrate military victories found their way into collections such as the "Book of Jashar" and the "Book of the Wars of YHWH," both of which are now missing.

With the development of the monarchy, the coronation of the king became one of the major events celebrated with music. At first, as in the cases of Absalom and Solomon, the *šôpār* was used to announce the actual event (2 Sam 15:10; 1 Kgs 1:34, 39, 41). The ensuing celebration was marked by music played on pipes (1 Kgs 1:40). Metal-made trumpets were more musically versatile than the ram's horn and, in addition to their use for signaling, were also used during celebrations (2 Kgs 11:14). Several of the psalms are considered enthronement psalms (Pss 2; 20; 68; 72; 89; 101; 110; 144) and were probably sung as part of the coronation celebration.

There is no question that musicians were part of the king's entourage (2 Sam 19:36 [Eng. 35]).[20] On various occasions, they probably entertained the king, his courtiers, and honored guests.

Not all occasions were happy. Some public performances included mourning for leaders (2 Sam 3:32–34) and lamentations (Judg 11:40).

RELIGIOUS OCCURRENCES. The numerous biblical references to music, musicians, dancing, and dancers engaged in cultic activities indicate that these artistic elements were well integrated into Israelite religious life. Cultic-related dances were either organized by the authorities or spontaneous as a result of religious fervor. Traditions of early dance and musical occurrences are connected with dancing around the golden calf (Exod 32:19), which was a spontaneous event. This type of spontaneous dancing is also presented in the story of David bringing the ark to Jerusalem (2 Sam 6:5, 14–15). Another type of cultic dancing that was supposed to influence the outcome of certain events is reflected in the dancing for Baal (1 Kgs 18:26–28), an act that was accompanied by the use of sharp instruments such as swords and lances to the point of the dancers wounding each other to elicit a divine response. Such dances are still practiced in certain Middle Eastern communities.

Music was used to set the mood for certain cultic practices, especially prophesying. One example of this is described in the encounter between Saul and the band of prophets (1 Sam 10:5). Upon hearing the music, Saul was seized "with prophetic rapture" and started acting like the other prophets. The instruments played by the group were the most common instruments: *nēbel* and *tôp*, *ḥālîl* and *kinnôr*. Another example of prophesying under the influence of music is that of Elisha (2 Kgs 3:15), who asked for a minstrel to come and play: "while the minstrel played, the power of YHWH came on Elisha."

With the establishment of the temple in Jerusalem, music performance at certain events became institutionalized. Singing and instrument playing became part of the ritual (Amos 5:23). Traditions maintain that David appointed the Levites to the temple as professional musicians and established the musicians' guilds (1 Chr 6:31; 15:16–24; 25:1) that continued to perform in the time of Josiah (2 Chr 35:15) and until the fall of the temple. Their descendants were among the returnees from the Babylonian exile (Ezra 2:41, 65), and they helped celebrate the inauguration of the temple: "the priests in their robes took their places with their trumpets, and the Levites, the sons of Asaph, with cymbals, to praise YHWH in the manner prescribed by King David of Israel" (Ezra 3:10).

Part of organized religion was the pilgrimages to shrines. Before the time of the monarchy, pilgrimages were made to local shrines (1 Sam 1:3, 21). With the centralization of the cult in Jerusalem,[21] pilgrims made their way there and on the way they sang (Songs of the Ascent, Pss 120–134).

VISUAL ARTS

The ancient Near East had a rich tradition of visual arts[22] that include drawing and painting, glyptic and plastic arts, ivory carving, metal and glass fashioning, and works in wood, clay, and other materials. Very little of what has been discovered at sites identified as Israelite can be labeled as authentic Israelite art, but this does not mean that the Israelites were not exposed to art objects.[23] With the exception of burnishing, Israelite pottery was plain, but Israel's neighbors produced exquisite pottery. During the Iron Age I, Philistine pottery was outstanding in its decorations, and in the Iron Age II Cypro-Phoenician pottery was the rage. Throughout the Israelite period, art objects were mostly the product of Phoenician artisans or were produced under Phoenician influence. Moreover, some of the inspiration for the Phoenician artists and artisans, as seen in the motifs and techniques they employed, came from neighboring cultures, mostly from Egypt. These include human figures with Egyptian elements such as gestures, but with narrower shoulders, and dressed in local garb.

IVORY

Large animal statues are well known from Late Bronze Palestine (e.g., from Hazor and Beth-shean), but none are known from the Iron Age. Similarly, large human statues are almost absent, but smaller figurines and plaques are found at many Iron Age sites. The most common material employed in making these objects was ivory, and ivory carving became the hallmark of Phoenician art. Ivory was used in making luxury items, including three-dimensional objects such as figurines, cosmetic paraphernalia, spindles and whorls, pendants, and knife handles, and in the production of inlaid furniture such as chairs (1 Kgs 10:18 = 2 Chr 9:17) or beds (Amos 6:4). One famous collection of ivories was found during the excavations at Samaria, and the pieces were probably used in furniture kept in the palace of the kings of Israel. A reference to such a place is made in 1 Kgs 22:39, where Ahab is said to have built "an ivory house (palace)" (*bêt haššēn*). According to Amos 3:15, there were several ivory palaces (see also Ps 45:9). That the kings of Israel and Judah were in possession of ivory objects is evident from Assyrian tribute and booty lists. Ivory objects were used for cultic purposes, as demonstrated by the ivory pomegranate mentioned earlier (see also below). Some of the common people also possessed ivory items such as combs, as is evident from archaeological finds in domestic structures.

The sources of ivory were elephant tusks and hippopotamus teeth. When ivory was not available, large bones were substituted.

CLAY

Clay was the most ubiquitous material for plastic art because of its availability and ease of manipulation. A unique object from the tenth century B.C.E. is that of the cultic clay stand from Taanach, which is a product of the Israelite-dominated region. The rectangular stand has four tiers with hand-fashioned scenes. Some scholars suggest that the bottom and third tiers portray Astarte, while the second and top tiers are devoted to YHWH. The bottom tier shows a female figurine flanked on each side by a lion. The second tier has a void in the middle flanked by a cherub (sphinx) on each side. In the middle of the third tier is depicted a tree of life flanked on each side by a horned ruminant (probably goats), and the top tier has in its center a horse with a winged sun disk. The scene at the top tier might be related to other depictions of horses in clay (see below and fig. 5.3).

Humanoid and zoomorphic figurines were part of the Israelite artistic inventory. Metal figurines were very few during the Israelite period. One example from the Early Iron Age is the bronze bull from the "Bull Site" in the Samaria Mountains. However, clay became a common material for the production of figurines, especially in the Iron Age II. The most common figurines found

Fig. 5.3. Taanach cult stand.
Courtesy Israel Antiquities Authority.

at Israelite sites belong to two groups, pillar figurines (see fig. 2.5) and horses with or without riders. The pillar figurines, sometimes referred to as Astarte figurines, are labeled so because their handmade body resembles a pillar with a flat bottom for standing. A few figurines have a body made on a potter's wheel. The pillar figurines are divided into two groups: those whose head with a curly hairdo was made in a mold and then attached to the body, and those whose head was made by pinching the top of the pillar to produce a birdlike face. Both sets of figurines display an exaggerated bust supported by the hands of the figurine. This feature made scholars propose that the figurines, whether depicting Astarte or not, were of a fertility goddess. The numerous biblical references to the Israelite worship of Astarte, whether in the temple or at home, lends credence to the suggestion that these figurines were the representation of the goddess Astarte and were used in home shrines. The worship of Astarte as a consort of YHWH is supported by inscriptions found at Kuntillet ʿAjrûd on the border of the Sinai and Negev and in Khirbet el-Qom in the Hebron area (see below and fig. 5.4).

Fig. 5.4. "Yhwh and his Asherah" inscription, Kuntillet ʿAjrûd.
By permission of Dr. Z. Meshel, TAU, excavator of the site.

Horse figurines are another type of common figurines found at Israelite sites. Some of the figurines still have or had a rider, and others display a disklike round object on top of the forehead between the ears. A suggestion has been made that the "disk" is a representation of the sun disk and that these horses are related to the worship mentioned in 2 Kgs 23:11: "He [Josiah] did away with the horses that the kings of Judah had set up in honor of the sun at the entrance to the house of YHWH ... and he burned the chariots of the sun."

Another cultic-related clay object, the remains of which are found at Israelite sites, is the "ashdoda"-type, or couch, figurine. A complete example is known from Philistine Ashdod, hence the name. It depicts a female with a long neck and small head whose body, which has no arms, turns at the hips into a couch or table. The number of these objects is quite limited, and most of the known remains are of the lower part, the couch.

GLYPTIC ART

Stone carving was relatively common in the Iron Age II. Israelite artisans were highly experienced in the production of stone objects such as scaraboid stamp seals, cosmetic palettes, and stone weights. Although the latter cannot be considered works of art, they attest to the proficiency of the Israelite stone artisans.

Most Israelite seals were made of precious or semiprecious stones, were shaped like a scarab, and could be worn on a string around the neck or set in a bezel in a ring. Seals were used to authenticate and verify documents (Jer 32:10–14, 44) or for identification (Gen 38:18). Most seals had the name of the owner in the top register separated by two or three straight lines from the name of his father below. Sometimes a third register was added with a title or a description of the owner's occupation, but at times this designation replaced the patronymic name. At times one of the registers has an illustration of an animate (e.g., rooster, lion) or inanimate (e.g., lyre, ship) object. All of that was enclosed in an oval frame made of one to three lines. Many of the known seals belonged to well-to-do individuals, scribes, court officials, and members of the royal family.[24]

Many lost seals are known by their impressions left in the clay, either on jar handles or bullae. The latter is a lump of clay applied to the string sealing a document, mostly papyrus. An important series of seal impressions, known as *lmlk* ("[belonging] to the king") impressions, is the result of a set of royal seals. The seals were impressed into the wet clay of jar handles, possibly verifying something related to the jar or its contents. These seals had the term *lmlk* inscribed in the top register and the name of one city out of four (Hebron, Ziph, Socoh, *mmšt*) in the bottom, with a depiction of either a flying scroll or a four-winged beetle in the middle. It has been suggested that the commodities in the sealed jars were related to Hezekiah's reforms and revolt against Assyria in 701 B.C.E.

Another series of stone-cut objects are cosmetic palettes. These circular, concave objects with a round depression in the center were made mostly of limestone. Most of them are decorated with simple designs arranged around the depression. Among the decorations are series of circles with a dot in the middle, circular grooves, and hatch marks. These palettes were most likely used by women to mix ingredients used for makeup.

MIXED MEDIA

Jewelry was another group of objects in which art found its expression. Granted, we do not know whether the objects were fashioned by Israelite artisans or were imported, but it is clear from archaeological finds and biblical references that Israelites adorned themselves with a variety of ornaments, including rings, necklaces, ear and nose rings, bracelets and anklets, and other objects, all of which were made of precious and semiprecious metals, stones, bones, shells, glass, and the like. Most of the jewelry recovered in archaeological excavations comes from burials where the objects were interred with the deceased.

Drawing and painting is another area for artistic expression that was carried out on a variety of materials, including stone and pottery. Most of the known drawings were done spontaneously and can be considered graffiti, using ink or scratching the picture into the solid material. There is a strong possibility that, as in the neighboring culture of Egypt, this artistic venue was also exercised on perishable materials such as wood, leather, papyrus, or parchment. Because of the nature of these materials and the climate, both of which did not permit their preservation, we lack any evidence. One example of this artistic endeavor is well attested by the ink on clay-jar drawings from the site of Kuntillet ʿAjrûd (see fig. 5.4). In addition to a few Hebrew inscriptions (see ch. 6), several jars bear the images of gods, people, animals, and plants.[25] Interestingly, one jar displays the image of the Egyptian god Bes with a second deity next to him. On the other side is a drawing of a woman playing a lyre. Also depicted are a lion, other animals, and a tree of life with an ibex on each side. Another drawing on the jar, that of a cow licking the tail of a suckling calf, is reminiscent of carved ivories from Nimrud and Arslan Tash. Among drawings on a second jar is one of a row of five standing people with raised arms in a gesture of prayer. While the execution of the drawing was by local artists, it is evident that they were highly influenced by the Syro-Phoenician artistic tradition. Since the inscriptions mention YHWH's name, it is safe to assume that the artists were also YHWH worshipers. In addition to the decorated jars, fragments of painted plaster suggest that the walls of the building were decorated with frescoes containing geometric and floral designs. The frescoes, found in association with the other artistic motifs, suggest that this art form was practiced not just in this isolated site.

FOR FURTHER STUDY

Braun, Joachim. *Music in Ancient Israel/Palestine: Archaeological, Written, and Comparative Sources.* Edited by David Noel Freedman. The Bible in Its World. Grand Rapids: Eerdmans, 2002.
This is the latest and most comprehensive treatment of the topic, covering it from the Stone Age through the Roman period (fourth century C.E.). It describes the variety of instruments played through the ages and the place music occupied in the different cultures of the region. Many illustrations accompany the text, followed by a exhaustive bibliography.

———. "Music, Musical Instruments." Pages 927–30 in *Eerdmans Dictionary of the Bible*. Edited by David Noel Freedman. Grand Rapids: Eerdmans, 2000.
A much shorter yet comprehensive version of the other work by the same author. A good, quick reference on the topic.

Frankfort, Henri. *The Art and Architecture of the Ancient Orient*. 4th ed. New Haven: Yale University Press, 1970.
Israelite art was at home with the art of the rest of the ancient Near East. While this work is devoted mostly to the art of Mesopotamia, it also pays attention to art in Anatolia, Egypt, Syria-Palestine, and ancient Persia. It contains over 440 black and white photographs and line drawings.

Gunter, Ann C. "Ancient Near Eastern Art." Pages 402–8 in vol. 1 of *Anchor Bible Dictionary*. Edited by David Noel Freedman. 6 vols. New York: Doubleday, 1992.
In this brief presentation, the art of Western Asia is examined from its earliest appearance to the fall of the Persian Empire. This survey includes not only a review of the various artistic expressions through the different periods but also a discussion of the discovery of ancient Near eastern art and the production of art in the ancient Near East.

6

WRITING—PRIVATE AND OFFICIAL

Were the Israelites literate, and, if yes, to what degree? It is difficult to determine how common reading and writing were among the Israelites. Furthermore, it is hard to gauge the changes in the level of literacy through the long Israelite period. Therefore, what follow are hints at what was possible, but no definite answers are given. Archaeological and written evidence suggest that, like Ammonite, Edomite, and Moabite, Hebrew, which used alphabetic script, was a dialect of West-Semitic (Canaanite). Hebrew writing was accomplished using the "Phoenician" script, which had twenty-two letters and could be used on many types of material, perishable and nonperishable. The dearth of written documents from the Israelite period is due mostly to the fact that much was written on perishables such as parchment, papyrus, and wood. What is available, besides the Hebrew Bible in its present form, was preserved on stone, precious metals, and in different forms of clay.

Writing was used for several purposes; therefore, the evidence can be classified into two groups: private and official. But who were the actual writers? Archaeological evidence suggests that there were private individuals who learned the art of writing and used it for their own purposes. Two of the earliest Hebrew documents, the abecedary from 'Izbet Sartah (ca. eleventh century B.C.E.) and the Gezer Calendar (ca. 925 B.C.E.), have been identified by several scholars as writing exercises. Both of these were scratched into a pottery sherd and a flat limestone fragment, respectively, and exhibit the product of untrained hands. Both documents point out that a certain amount of writing was taking place among individual Israelites.[1] The case of 'Izbet Sartah is most interesting because it pertains to a small hamlet where one would not expect any literacy. The existence of the abecedary indicates that at least two people at this rural settlement were capable of writing, the student and teacher.

Biblical and archaeological evidence indicates that there was a well-trained class of people who were known as scribes (*sôpərîm;* sg. *sôpēr*). In early Israelite history they were official recorders of events (Judg 5:14), and with the development of the monarchy, an official scribe was appointed as a member of the bureaucracy (2 Sam 8:17). Scribes helped with transactions in the temple (Jer 36:10) and assisted some of the prophets in recording their words (Jer 36:18, 32). Scribes were employed by officials to tend to official correspondence and provided services to individuals who needed help with the same. How exactly they were trained is not known. From comparisons with the neighboring cultures, we can assume that scribes were an organized group and were trained in centers such as the temples and royal palaces by copying certain works.

Written evidence can be found inscribed on pottery sherds, incised in jars or jar fragments before or after firing, stamped on jars and jar handles, and incised in rock or metal.[2] When examining written evidence, it is sometimes hard to determine whether to classify it as for private or public (official) use. Some items can be classified as both, but for the purpose of presentation of the evidence I will present them here in a certain order.

PRIVATE

Objects that have writing on them will be classified here as private if they were produced for the benefit of an individual without expectations of compensation from the public sector. Under this classification we can identify several items, including amulets and requests for blessings and other inscriptions of a personal nature.

Some of these materials were mentioned before, including the Gezer Calendar and the abecedaries from ʿIzbet Sartah and Kuntillet ʿAjrûd. To these should be added the requests from Kuntillet ʿAjrûd and Khirbet el-Qom beseeching "YHWH and his Asherah" to bless certain individuals.[3] The silver amulets from the burial caves at Ketef Hinnom in Jerusalem, dated to the early sixth century B.C.E., belong to the same group. One of them contains a text very close to the priestly blessing of Num 6:24–26 and reads: "May YHWH bless you and watch over you! May YHWH make his face shine upon you and grant you peace!" Another burial-related inscription from the Silwan cemetery in Jerusalem is known as the Royal Steward Inscription. It reads: "This is [the tomb of …]yahu, the royal steward [ʾăšer ʿal habbayit]. There is [he]re no silver or gold, [on]ly [his bones] and the bon[es] of his maid-servant. Cursed be the one who opens it!" Following the reference in Isa 22:15–16, it has been suggested that this is the tomb of Shebna, who was "over the house" in Hezekiah's administration (eighth–seventh century B.C.E.). The cemetery in Silwan yielded several other inscriptions related to burials, all of which suggest the ability of common people to read, since these inscriptions were meant for them.

A quite common writing material was pottery, whole or fragmentary, known as ostraca (sg. ostracon). One very famous ostracton is the letter from Meṣad (Fortress) Hashavyahu found at Yavneh-Yam south of Tel Aviv

and dated to the seventh century B.C.E. (fig. 6.1). Although
this letter is addressed to the
governor (ḥaśśār), which may
define it as an official document, it contains a plea of an
individual trying to reclaim his
personal property (cloak) con-
fiscated by another official
named Hashavyahu for not
completing the harvest of his
assigned daily quota of grain.
The document does not have
the name of the addressee or
the name of the plaintiff, and it
has been suggested that this is
due to the fact that the com-
plaint was drafted at the
entrance to the fort and the
plaintiff was waiting by the
door for the answer. Furthermore, the language of the letter
suggests that it was dictated in a

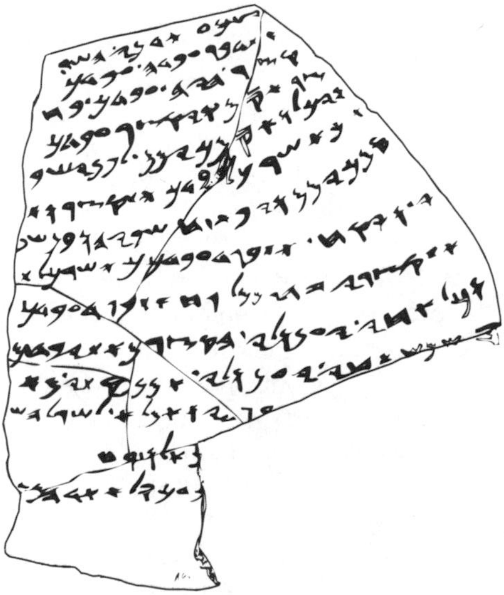

Fig. 6.1. Drawing of a judicial
petition from Meṣad Hashavyahu.
Courtesy Andrew G. Vaughn.

hurry and that the claim probably relies on the law stated in Exod 22:25–26
(Eng. 26–27; see also Deut 24:12–13): "If you take your neighbor's cloak in
pledge, return it to him by sunset, because it is his only covering. It is the
cloak in which he wraps himself. In what else shall he sleep?"

Other written evidence such as inscriptions on jars describing their
contents or their owners reflects the fact that there were quite a few individuals who, during the time of the divided monarchy, were familiar with
alphabetical writing.

OFFICIAL WRITINGS

Earlier I pointed out that for official business scribes were employed
in the royal court, in the temples and shrines, and by several of the
prophets. Being a scribe was considered belonging to an elevated class.
Biblical references show that some of the scribes were well connected.
One of the duties of scribes was to assist in keeping official records and
maintaining correspondence. There are good examples for both of these
functions. One such example is that of Jeremiah, who bought a tract of
land and recorded the purchase in a sealed document, which was given to
his scribe for safekeeping (Jer 32:6–15).

CORRESPONDENCE

Letter writing and archive keeping had a long tradition in the ancient Near East. Correspondence archives have been found in Mesopotamia, Syria, Egypt, and Anatolia. Letters in ancient Israel were written on perishable (papyrus, leather) and nonperishable (sherds) materials. In spite of the nature of these materials, evidence for the former is found in the large number of bullae found at various sites, especially in Jerusalem. Bullae (sg. bulla), which are small lumps of clay that sealed the knot of a thong tying a rolled-up papyrus or parchment document, were impressed with a seal to protect the document from being opened by an unauthorized person (see fig. 6.2).[4] Their recovery is a safe marker for the past existence of perishable documents in the loci where they were discovered. Since almost all of them bear inscriptions, the seal impressions, in addition to actual seals, are an excellent source for the study of the Israelite and non-Israelite onomasticon, the administration, and the histories and relationships of certain individuals. Although the documents were lost due to fire or other destructive conditions, their former existence is well attested. Unfortunately, the content cannot be recovered.

Fig. 6.2. Drawing of a seal from Arad. Courtesy Andrew G. Vaughn.

Some of the seals and seal impressions yield not only names of individuals and their family lineage but also some of the occupations and social standings of the seal owners. In addition to people in positions such as manservant (na'ar), scribe, priest, doctor, high official ('ebed), we know of particular individuals who served as "over the house" (royal steward, 1 Kgs 4:6), "over the corvée" (2 Sam 20:24; 1 Kgs 5:28 [Eng. 5:14]), "governor of the city" (śar hā'îr, 1 Kgs 22:26; 2 Kgs 23:8), "son of the king" (ben hammelek), and "daughter of the king" (bat hammelek). We have also seals and seal impressions with the names of Kings Ahaz and Hezekiah.[5]

Although no papyrus or parchment documents survived from the Israelite period, a number of ostraca survived and are instructive concerning certain aspects of life. Ostraca recovered at a site can shed light not only on life there but also on other sites and individuals connected to it during the period of their composition. Letters written on pottery sherds were found in the fortress of Arad, located east of Beer-sheba, and at the city gate of Lachish, located in the southern Shephelah. Arad provides us with ostraca from several periods, with one collection of about twenty dated to ca. 597 B.C.E. and belonging to the archive of Elyashib, probably the commander of the fort. As Klaas Smelik suggests, the number of ostraca in the archive is small because Elyashib kept them for a short period until they could be transcribed to the official record, which was probably kept on papyrus.[6] The archive, dating to the last days of Arad before falling into the hands of the Babylonians, describes daily activities such as the disbursement of rations to individuals or to an entity named *kittim,* probably a group of Cypriot mercenaries. One of the ostraca, number 18, mentions "the house of YHWH," probably the Jerusalem temple. Moreover, it has been suggested that the reference is to either the Jerusalem temple or the one in Arad,[7] but by that time the Arad temple was no longer functioning as a result of Hezekiah's reforms.

The other group of ostraca, known as the Lachish letters, is dated to the final days of the kingdom of Judah (ca. 587/586 B.C.E.). Because they are repetitious and were written on sherds mostly belonging to the same jar, it has been suggested by Yigael Yadin that the Lachish letters were drafts composed before a final version on papyrus was prepared and dispatched. The ostraca were written by Hoshayah to Ya'osh and invoke the name of YHWH in the greetings and throughout the text. Letter number 4 is most interesting because it mentions the fact that the fire signals of Azekah, a neighboring site to the north, could no longer be seen (see fig. 6.3). Fire signals are mentioned in Jer 6:1, and the final days of Judah are mentioned in 34:7, when "the army of the king of Babylon was attacking Jerusalem and the remaining towns in Judah, namely, Lachish and Azekah, the only fortified towns left there." The Lachish letters, and especially letter no. 4, provide a physical link to the events described in Jeremiah.

Fig. 6.3. Drawing of Lachish Letter 4.
Courtesy Andrew G. Vaughn.

RECORD KEEPING

One of the functions of the bureaucracy was to keep records, some of which related to the economy in general and to tax collection in particular.

One example for this activity is provided by the Samaria ostraca, a collection of tax receipts dated to the eighth century B.C.E. (probably to the reign of Jeroboam II, ca. 787–746 B.C.E.) discovered in one of the rooms of the royal palace in Samaria. The ostraca contain dates of receipt—the ninth year, tenth year, fifteenth year, and even seventeenth year, probably to the reign of a king—with the name of the receiver, the commodity (wine or oil), and the place of origin, which was either a private or royal estate, as is demonstrated for example in ostracon 18: "In the tenth year. From Hazeroth to Gaddiyau. A jar of fine oil."[8]

Another example of record keeping, which I mentioned earlier in a different context, is that of the *lmlk* stamped jar handles. These impressions bear the inscription *lmlk* ("[belonging] to the king"), a depiction of a four-winged beetle or a two-winged flying scroll, and the name of one of four places: Hebron, Socoh, Ziph, and *mmšt*. It has been suggested that the latter name is a designation for Jerusalem. Through archaeological excavations, especially at Lachish, it has been established that the *lmlk* jars belong to the reign of King Hezekiah, and it has been suggested that they were part of Hezekiah's reforms and played a role in the preparation for his revolt in 701 B.C.E. against the Assyrian King Sennacherib. How the jars were used is not completely clear, but one suggestion is that the jars contained commodities such as oil and wine and were used in the provisioning of the places that were supposed to participate in the revolt. Another proposal based on the study of the *lmlk* handles and their provenience opposes the narrow approach to the use of these jars for preparations just before the siege and offers that they were used during a much longer period. Accordingly, Hezekiah started issuing commodities in these jars as soon as he stopped paying tribute to Assyria and anticipated an attack by Sennacherib.[9] A third suggestion is that the commodities were used in part to ameliorate the economic conditions of the priests who were deposed by Hezekiah's reforms to secure their loyalty during the revolt.[10] Since many of the *lmlk* jars had on their handles impressions of seals belonging to Judean officials,[11] it is quite possible that the stamped and similar jars were recorded by the king's administration before being shipped out to their final destination.

CHRONICLES

Israelite culture had a variety of ways for official documentation. Letters would be written in draft form and then transcribed to an official document made of papyrus or parchment that would be transmitted to the addressee. Similarly, notes would be taken and a variety of lists kept first in draft form to be later transcribed to the official record stored in archives. An important category of official records was that of chronicles, "the book of memorable events, the chronicle" (Esth 6:1). From numerous parenthetical statements in the Bible, it appears that much of the historical recorded recollections are based on source books that were kept probably in the archives at the royal courts. Many times there are specific references to these books. The Annals of the Kings of Judah are said to have records of the deeds of most of the individual kings. These records must have served as references when the text we read today was originally written. Reports of the existence of such records relate to Rehoboam (1 Kgs 14:29), Abijam (1 Kgs 15:7), Asa (1 Kgs 15:23), Jehoshaphat (1 Kgs 22:46), Jehoram (2 Kgs 8:23), Jehoash (2 Kgs 12:20), Amaziah (2 Kgs 14:18), Azariah (2 Kgs 15:6), Jotham (2 Kgs 15:36), Ahaz (2 Kgs 16:19), Hezekiah (2 Kgs 20:20), Manasseh (2 Kgs 21:17), Amon (2 Kgs 21:25), Josiah (2 Kgs 23:28), and Jehoiakim (2 Kgs 24:5). The Bible does not report that such records existed for Jehoahaz, Jehoiakin, and Zedekiah; this is probably because of the circumstances surrounding the end of their reign.

There was a similar archive for the kings of Israel. The Bible mentions that the following kings had an entry in the Annals of the Kings of Israel: Nadab (1 Kgs 15:31), Elah (1 Kgs 16:14), Omri (1 Kgs 16:27), Ahab (1 Kgs 22:39), Ahaziah (2 Kgs 1:18), Jehu (2 Kgs 10:34), Jehoahaz (2 Kgs 13:8), Jehoash (2 Kgs 14:15), Jeroboam II (2 Kgs 14:28), Zechariah (2 Kgs 15:11), Shallum (2 Kgs 15:15), Menahem (2 Kgs 15:21), Pekahiah (2 Kgs 15:26), and Pekah (2 Kgs 15:31). Hoshea son of Elah, who was the last king of the northern kingdom, is not mentioned as having an entry in the annals, obviously because of the destruction and extinction of the kingdom.

MONUMENTAL INSCRIPTIONS

Ancient Israel is not known for producing monumental or dedicatory inscriptions. While Israel's neighbors produced inscriptions such as the Mesha Inscription (or Moabite Stone), the Dan Inscription, and the Tel Miqne-Ekron Inscription, there is only one inscription from ancient Israel that can be considered as such, the Siloam Inscription, and even this inscription is different from other monumental inscriptions because the place where it was found, in Hezekiah's (or the Siloam) Tunnel, was hidden and out of the public eye. The inscription reads:

> [ ] the tunnel. And this was the story of the tunnel. While [the stonecutters were] still [striking with] the axe, each man toward his fellow, and while there were still three cubits to be cut [through, there was heard] the voice of a man calling to his fellow, as there was a crack [*zdh*] in the rock, to the right [and to the left]. And on the day of (the breakthrough of) the tunnel, the stonecutters struck each toward his fellow, axe against [a]xe. And the water ran from the source to the pool for 1,200 cubits. And one hundred cubits was the height of the rock above the head(s) of the stonecutters.

The place where the inscription was found indicates that it was not intended for public view. The absence of the name of the king (presumably Hezekiah) who ordered this project suggests that the inscription was not ordered by the king but followed the initiative of the workers. If this is correct, we can assume that reading and writing were common in the eighth century B.C.E. This point is strengthened by the existence of the three foreign inscriptions mentioned above and by the "Over the House" tomb inscription, all of which were directed at ordinary people.

MISCELLANEOUS INSCRIPTIONS

We cannot enumerate all the inscriptions extant today, mostly because they are too numerous and very brief. However, I would like to mention again a group of objects, the Judean stone weights, many of which are inscribed. These dome-shaped objects were used as weights in daily commerce, and many of them have an inscription at the top indicating their weight (denomination). Some weights bear the inscriptions *bqʿ, pym, nṣp,* or a sign similar to the Greek letter gamma (probably denoting shekel) with an Egyptian hieratic number symbol of 5, 10, 20, 30, or 40 next to it.

One very important inscription that needs to be mentioned here is known as the Pomegranate Inscription because it appears on the shoulder of a pomegranate-shaped ivory object. The object has a hole in the bottom as if it were supposed to be placed on a scepter. The inscription is damaged and incomplete. The object's place of origin is unknown, but scholars assume that it originally was in use in the Jerusalem temple. This relies on the proposal of how to complete the inscription: *qdš khnm lby[t yhw]h,* "Holy to the priests, belonging to the house [of YHW]H."

CREATIVE WRITING

Several books of the Bible serve as a good example for the existence of creative writing that produced writings not necessarily anchored in history, politics, the legal system, and other types of formal writing. Books in this category belong to philosophical musing, wisdom literature, poetry, and such. Several of these works survived and found their way into the Bible. However, from biblical references it seems that ancient Israel was highly creative in its writings, though unfortunately many of the works have not survived. The Book of Jashar, mentioned in Josh 10:13 and 2 Sam 1:18, was a book of poetry that did not survive. Another book of poetry, now extinct, is the Book of the Wars of YHWH (Num 21:14), probably devoted to the celebration of Israel's wars and victories.

Creative writing in ancient Israel is proof to the fact that during the Israelite period there were people educated in writing and reading who had enough leisure time to devote to such creativity.

For Further Study

Avigad, Nahman. *Bullae and Seals from a Post-Exilic Judean Archive.* Qedem 4. Jerusalem: Institute of Archaeology, Hebrew University of Jerusalem, 1976.

————. *Hebrew Bullae from the Time of Jeremiah: Remnants of a Burnt Archive.* Jerusalem: Israel Exploration Society, 1986.

Avigad, Nahman, and Benjamin Sass. *Corpus of West Semitic Stamp Seals.* Jerusalem: Israel Academy of Sciences and Humanities; Israel Exploration Society; Institute of Archaeology, Hebrew University of Jerusalem, 1997.

All three books make up an excellent compilation of the majority of known seals and seal impressions from the Iron Age. This series of studies presents an onomasticon, lists of titles and professions, all of which provide the background for the study of Israelite society and culture.

McCarter, P. Kyle, Jr. *Ancient Inscriptions: Voices from the Biblical World.* Washington, D.C.: Biblical Archaeology Society, 1996.

This work is a companion to the slide set "Ancient Near Eastern Inscriptions" produced by the Biblical Archaeology Society. The description of each slide in the set contains historical background and interpretation. Some descriptions include excellent line drawings. Areas covered are Egypt and Syria-Palestine.

Smelik, Klaas A. D. *Writings from Ancient Israel: A Handbook of Historical and Religious Documents.* Louisville: Westminster John Knox, 1991.

An excellent presentation of the most famous and important inscriptions from the Israelite period. Some of the texts included are the Gezer Calendar, Moabite Stone, and ostraca from Samaria, Arad, and Lachish. Each presentation includes historical background and interpretation of the inscription.

Vaughn, Andrew G. *Theology, History, and Archaeology in the Chronicler's Account of Hezekiah.* Society of Biblical Literature Archaeology and Biblical Studies 4. Atlanta: Scholars Press, 1999.

This study looks at the Chronicler's account of Hezekiah and integrates it with extrabiblical data. It concludes that the Chronicler, in spite of being interested in presenting an ideologically laden message, was interested in writing history.

7

A DAY IN THE LIFE OF THE AHUZAM FAMILY

These are the days of King Hezekiah.[1] It is summer time, and the barley harvest is almost over while the wheat harvest is about to begin. Two years earlier, the great revolt against Assyria took place, and King Sennacherib, in his fury, devastated most of the country. Most of Judah lies in ruins, and with the exception of the countryside, life in the few remaining cities is very hard.

Shmaryahu son of Jotham son of Aminadab son of Ahiel son of Nur, who belongs to the Ahuzam family of the tribe of Judah, is living in the small hamlet of Ether, located in the district of Socho not far from Maresha. Here he was born, and, when the time comes, he would like to be buried in his family plot.

Ether is made of four house complexes surrounded by a low wall built to contain the livestock, all of which are situated at the top of a rolling, limestone hill with stepped, rocky slopes (see fig. 7.1). Terraces planted with grape vines and olive trees gird the slopes. These are the products of hard, cooperative work, which took generations to accomplish and were passed from one generation to another as was mandated by custom and law. Other fruit trees such as figs and pomegranates grow closer to the houses, with vegetable beds interspersed in between. The cereal fields stretch at the foot of the hill all around and can be watched from the hamlet. Inhabitants of Ether are fortunate, since their lands are very close to home, and not much time has to be wasted in travel to and fro. At the foot of the hill in the middle of the dry wadi bed, a stone-lined well surrounded with stone-carved troughs serves as the main water source. The rocky slopes are poke-marked with water cisterns carved in bedrock, and a small cemetery containing seven or eight family burial caves occupies the northeast slope just outside the hamlet. Close to the terraced vineyards and groves, the rocky slopes host a variety of installations such as watchtowers and wine and olive presses. Closer to the hamlet, on a leveled area open to the western breeze, the threshing floor is the most impressive feature.

In the days of the revolt, Ether was under the protection and jurisdiction of the great city of Lachish. But Lachish was conquered and destroyed by Sennacherib, and only recently it was announced that King Hezekiah has been contemplating rebuilding it. Presently, most of the Judean population is living unmolested in villages because the Assyrians appreciate the fact that the inhabitants can produce agricultural by-products, which are brought to Assyria on a yearly basis as tribute.

Shmaryahu, married to Hodiah from the Garmi family of the tribe of Judah and originally from nearby Keilah, is a successful farmer. His family

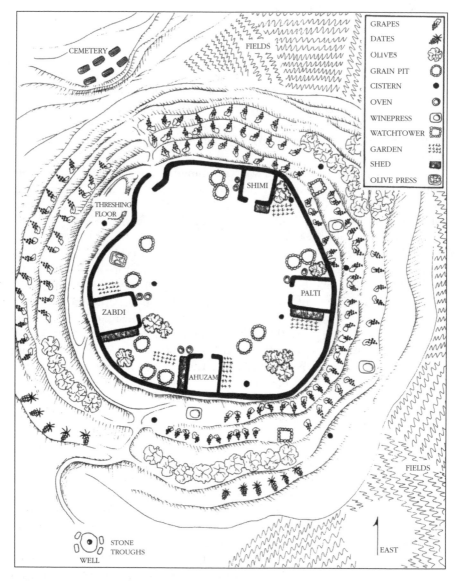

Fig. 7.1. Village map. Drawing by Dylan Karges.

has been in this location for many generations. Tradition has it that they
received the land as an allotment right after the conquest of Canaan led by
the legendary Joshua son of Nun. The real story is more complicated, but
the tradition is still upheld by the family. Shmaryahu, the eldest son of his
parents Jotham and Bathya, inherited the land and the agricultural know-
how and was willing to defend it against all enemies and preserve it for
his oldest son, who will inherit it at the right time.

Shmaryahu lives with his wife, two sons (Zechariah, 13; Obadiah, 15)
and a daughter (Abigail, 16), in a two-storied pillared house (see fig. 7.1).
Another son and daughter died when they were still babies. With them live
also his elderly parents, who can no longer work in the fields, and his
younger brother Malkiel, who is married to Zeruiah and has two children,
a son (Joash, 10) and daughter (Tamar, 12).

Two of the other building complexes in Ether belong to the Judahite
families Shimi and Palti, who were close relatives of the Ahuzam family
as well as of the Garmi family. The Shimites and Paltites have been settled in Ether as long as the Ahuzamites, and often they intermarried.
Actually, Zeruiah was of the Palti family and Bathya of the Shimi family.
Such close relationship made for close cooperation among the inhabitants
of Ether when help was needed in certain situations, such as building and
maintaining terraces, constructing additions to the houses, cleaning the
cisterns before the winter rains, and seasonal chores such as harvesting
and processing the produce.

The house of the Ahuzam family is a typical pillared house no different from the other houses in Ether or the neighboring villages. Jotham and
his father Aminadab were quite successful in all their endeavors and managed to amass property and livestock, all of which is reflected in the
Ahuzam compound and is now controlled and managed by Shmaryahu.
The two-storied house has several adjoining additions where some of the
livestock, especially the two oxen, a large ram, and fattened calves, are
kept, as well as some of the farming equipment. The house has strong
stone foundations with a mud-brick superstructure and ceilings made of
beams, overlaid with branches, reeds, and mud plaster. The house is
entered through a wide, two-winged, wooden door that can be bolted
from the inside. It opens onto the broad space in the middle of the hamlet. Inside, two rows of stone pillars (monoliths) divide the ground floor
into three long rooms with a broadroom at their back. The central room is
mostly kept vacant, while the two side rooms and the broadroom have narrow, low walls that divide them into several activity areas. A few of the
small rooms have jars stacked next to and on top of each other. Most of
them contain wine and oil. A few are full with grain, though the family
prefers to keep most of the grain stored in bulk in their stone-lined, plastered storage pits just outside the house. The commodities stored in the jars

are for use in daily food preparation. In the winter, one corner room is used to keep the two family donkeys, while the other corner room is for keeping the small herd of sheep and goats. Both rooms are cobbled and have wooden and stone troughs. When the animals are kept in these rooms, the floor is usually covered with straw. One of the small rooms is full of fodder, while another one is occupied by a vertical loom.

A domed bread oven occupies one of the corners of the central room, while the other corner has an open cooking hearth. A large grinding installation is set near the bread oven. For summer cooking, similar installations are located just outside the house.

The second floor is reached by a ladder leaned against one of the sides of a large opening in the ceiling that covers the ground floor. The roof is considered the third floor because it is used as a living space and can be reached in the same manner. The room arrangement on the second floor mirrors the arrangement of the ground floor, though without the small dividing walls. One adult couple and their children occupy each of the side rooms, and the grandparents live in the back room. The central space in the middle of the floor is used for communication between the rooms and as a place of assembly where the family meets for their common meals and where other social activities take place.

The flat roof is considered a living space and is used as such in the summer. The cool breezes make this space a favorite place where family members can sleep away from the heat of the rooms below. Temporary booths with covers made of branches and reeds provide some shelter from the heat of the day and the dews at night. Certain areas of the roof are used seasonally for drying fruit such as grapes and figs. The edge of the roof has a parapet to protect people from falling off. During the winter, rainwater is collected on the flat roof and directed through a drain to a cistern below.

It is summer, and the days are long and hot. It is important to start the day early, even before sunrise. If the workers get going at dawn, they can be in the field with first light. Hodiah and Zeruiah get up first. Their biological clocks awaken them before dawn, when it is still dark. Hodiah gets up and lights two oil lamps, one for her and one for Zeruiah, who goes down to the ground floor to light the fuel in the bread oven. Hodiah follows Zeruiah quietly and goes into the storeroom, where she collects a measure of flour, a small amount of oil, and some water from the large jar standing by the door. The flour was ground in the afternoon of the previous day, and the water was fetched also during the previous day. She puts it all in a large bowl, mixes it well, and kneads it into dough. There is no time for the dough to rise, so Hodiah and Zeruiah make small, flat cakes and place them on round, rough clay trays to be placed in the oven for baking. As soon as the oven is hot, they place the trays one by one in the oven. While Zeruiah stays in charge of baking, Hodiah picks up some of the vegetables she harvested in the garden the previous day. These include cucumbers and onions. She also breaks a few pieces off the large hunk of dry cheese.

To make sure that the day will be successful, Hodiah goes into the house shrine, which is located in a corner of one of the small side rooms, and makes a small offering on a limestone block standing in front of the clay figurine of the goddess Astarte. Shmaryahu does not approve of this custom, but it was done in her family for generations, and she does not see any reason to stop now. By that time, sounds are being heard from the roof, where the rest of the family is waking up and getting ready to face the day after consuming the morning meal. One by one they come down by the ladder; they go down all the way to the ground floor to wash their face and hands. They do it over a bowl so they can conserve the water for the garden and the animals. Then they climb back to the second floor and sit in a circle in the middle of the floor, where it is open to the sky. Hodiah and Zeruiah hasten up by the ladder from the ground floor, bringing with them the freshly baked bread and the vegetables. Hodiah goes down one more time and brings up a skin full of yogurt and pours it into several small bowls that are used as drinking vessels.

The meal is eaten in haste because no one wants to waste time on empty chatter. They would rather be in the fields in the cool of the day than waste time. The roles are well rehearsed and known, and there is no need for special instructions or reminders. While the field workers eat their meal, Hodiah and Zeruiah pack the midday meals for them to pick up and go. By this time, Jotham and Bathya have joined the family. They are eating the morning meal with the rest of the family, and they also are getting ready to face their chores, which they carry out around the house. The family cannot afford having around any idle hands.

The meal is over. Shmaryahu, Malkiel, Zechariah, and Obadiah grab their goat-skin bags containing the midday meal and another large water skin and go down to the ground floor to get the donkeys ready for the day. They harness the animals and put on their backs a cover that is supposed to protect them from getting scratched by the heavy loads of stalks. They put water in the stone troughs and some fodder in the wooden troughs for the animals while Abigail and Tamar join them on the ground floor to milk the sheep and goats before going to the pasture. Jotham arrives from the second floor to help Abigail and Tamar in milking the ewes by grabbing them by the head and holding them in place while they are being milked into a large open bowl. When milking is over, the young lambs and kids are allowed to join their mothers for a short nursing session. Bathya brings two bags with packed meals for the girls to take on their hike with the herd. They unhook a goatskin container and fill it up with water. Each also picks up a pouch with personal items. After separating the mothers from their kids, they are ready to leave at the same time as the four males are ready to go to the field. Their sheep dog yelps with excitement, knowing that he will be getting out of the house shortly.

Hodiah and Zeruiah each gets a medium-sized water jar with a narrow neck and goes out the door with the others. They will accompany the girls to the well, and before drawing water to take to the house, they will help them water the sheep and goats. Bathya goes back to the roof and tidies up the bedding while Jotham puts the ground floor in order. Joash joins his grandfather in cleaning the ground floor; his main chore is collecting dung that can be used for fuel and other purposes, such as fertilizing the garden. When Bathya is done straightening the roof area, she goes to the second floor to sweep it and collects the used bowls so they can be washed on the ground floor. When Jotham and Joash finish cleaning the ground floor, they bring some mashed grain mixed with a little milk to feed the lambs and kids. They are trying to wean them slowly, slowly so the ewes will have more milk left for processing.

By this time the two women and the two girls reach the well. Going downhill is easy for everybody. The shepherds from the Palti and Shimi families have started to congregate at the well. Water is drawn for the animals on a first-come-first-served basis, which is a good reason to start early. The Ahuzamites are lucky today; they came second and will be able to get their animals watered soon, then draw water to take home to fill up the large jars standing by the door and serving as water containers for daily use. It will take more than one trip to fill them up. This is another good reason to get to the well early, since climbing back uphill when it is hot is not a pleasant chore.

The shepherds by the well are mostly female because during the cereal harvest season most of the males are busy in the fields. The meeting by the well is always a social occasion for exchange of gossip and news. When young males are present, they usually eye the girls, while the latter bashfully turn their faces away, though not before getting a glimpse of the young men. This is an opportunity for the unmarried to get to know each other and maybe form some kind of an attraction that can later be transmitted by their fathers, who would meet to discuss an arranged marriage.

When Abigail and Tamar are done watering their small herd, they start on their daily circuit while Hodiah and Zeruiah fill up their jars and start climbing back to the hamlet. It will take them four to five trips before the large jars are full.

***

The four Ahuzam males have reached their destination, where they are joined by a few itinerant hired hands who will help them with the harvest.

These people are mostly refugees of the war against the Assyrians. Their homes in the villages were sacked, and they and their families live in some natural caves that provide them with shelter. While they are mostly concerned with their immediate survival, they hope someday to return to and rebuild their villages.

Each of the adults has a sickle: Shmaryahu and Malkiel each owns an iron sickle, while the hired workers, who are poor, have sickles made of flint blades placed in a wooden heft and held there with bitumen. Everyone is well trained and capable of handling the different tasks involved in the harvest. This way they can switch before they get tired of doing a particular task. The order of tasks cannot be changed. The harvesters go first and, after grabbing a handful of stalks, cut them with a sickle as close to the ground as possible. No matter how close it might be, there is always something left for the herd to graze on. The sheaf collectors come next and collect the small bunches left by the harvesters into large sheaves, which they tie around with one or two stalks. The sheaves are taken to the edge of the field, where they are bunched together and tied to the backs of the donkeys, which are led to the threshing floor. Each family at Ether has its marked space at the threshing floor for keeping the stalks before they are threshed.

Shmaryahu and Malkiel supervise the work. They set the harvesting pace, make sure that the sheaves are tightly tied, and ensure that the load is well balanced on the donkeys and will not topple off when the donkeys go uphill. They tie the load to the backs of the donkeys with ropes made of goat hair. Obadiah and Zechariah are the donkey drivers. Once the animals are loaded, they take them on the beaten track to the threshing floor. It is not an easy task because it is important to make sure that the donkeys do not stray from the path and that the load does not slip off the donkeys' backs. In addition, when they arrive at the threshing floor, they need to unload the sheaves in the proper place. Going up the hill several times a day is quite tiring. Luckily, they can ride the donkeys back to the field, and they relish this opportunity to have some donkey races.

The heat of the day and the cutting of the stalks bring out swarms of little gnats that continue to bother the harvesters in spite of their attempts to drive them away with long swipes of their hands. The temperature is rising steadily, and the workers wipe the sweat from their brows with the edge of their headgear. The workers wear tunics that reach to their knees and are held in place with belts made of goat hair; a wrapped-around piece of cloth covers the head of each worker. It is important to set a pace and to keep it as long as possible. Usually the workers can do so until they break for the midday meal. At this time, they all gather under a large, shady tree. Today it is a solitary terebinth on a small rise. The area around the tree and the lower branches have been cleared by the sheep and goats.

They wait for the boys to return from their trip to the threshing floor before breaking for the meal. They will spend enough time under the tree not just to eat but for their bodies to cool down.

An "unofficial" group of workers present in the field during harvest is the gleaners. They always go behind the reapers and sheaf collectors picking up individual stocks that somehow are left behind and do not make it into the sheaf. Not being part of the family, they are not invited to join the harvesters at their midday meal, so they find a place away from them where they can consume their meal. The gleaners will stay in the field late after the harvesters have left in the hope that a sheaf will be left behind, thus becoming theirs according to the stated law of gleaning.

Obadiah and Zechariah are back from their second trip of the day to the threshing floor. In spite of the fact that they rode back on donkey back, they are tired, hungry, and thirsty. When they are back and sitting under the tree, the food is unpacked. Today's menu is similar to yesterday's and not different from what it will be tomorrow: flat bread, onion, cucumber, field greens, and herbs. They also have two small juglets, one filled with olive oil and the other with vinegar, both for dipping the bread. Water from the skin is their thirst-quenching drink. Malkiel strikes a flint against his sickle, producing a spark that catches a small pile of straw lying in the middle of a small stone circle, and a smoky fire leaps out. He maintains the fire by adding more bits of straw and small branches. He takes a few barley heads, which he brought with him from the field, and one by one he rubs them between his hands. The dry grain falls out on top of a concaved piece of broken pottery, which in turn he places in the fire and makes parched grain. When this is ready, Malkiel pulls it out carefully from the fire and passes it around for everyone to take some and nibble. He repeats this a few times until they are all full and ready to take a brief nap.

**

After leaving the well, Abigail and Tamar take their position at the head of the herd, encouraging the animals to follow them with soft calls and whistles. They entice the lead ewe to follow them by offering her bits of dry bread. The other sheep and goats with their herd instincts follow the leader. Their black and white spotted dog continuously circles the herd to keep it together. As they walk up a hill following their daily route, the girls talk about all sorts of things. Abigail is of marrying age, so part of the conversation is about her attraction to one of the young Shimi boys. He was not at the well today, but she gets to see him every so often when he comes to the well to help his sister. However, the girls cannot afford to continue this chat without doing something productive.

Abigail takes out from her pouch a hunk of wool from the latest crop. The sheep were shorn just recently in preparation for the summer heat and produced a large amount of wool that needs to be spun into yarn, which can then be woven into cloth. She fishes out of the bottom of her pouch a spindle with a pottery whorl stuck on it, attaches a few strands of wool to its elongated end, and starts spinning. She holds the mass of wool in her armpit, and with her fingers she pulls and twists the strands while spinning the spindle to produce a long yarn, which she wraps around the spindle handle. Tamar follows suit. She is not as accomplished a spinner as Abigail, but she is "in training," and whatever she can produce is welcomed in the household.

The girls reach their destination, a hill covered with dry grasses and wilted flowers, topped with an oak tree, under which they take shelter from the hot sun. The sheep and goats continue to move while grazing, and the dog keeps them close and from straying away. Whenever a single animal tries to get away from the flock, one of the girl throws a stone that lands on the outside of the animal and prompts it to return to the group. The dog is well aware of these attempts, and when the stone lands and startles the animal, he is there to bite its ankle and convince it to point its nose in the right direction.

The girls have been spinning quite a yarn, and Abigail feels the need for a break. She takes out of her pouch a flute made of reed and prepares to play A few days ago, while sitting with the family after the evening meal, her grandfather Jotham taught her a lively melody that she has been practicing whenever she has a chance. It was a familiar song, and both she and Tamar knew the lyrics, so Tamar joins her and sings along. They go through the routine three times, then Abigail starts playing another song. The girls have fun for a short while, but the herd needs their attention. The flock has been moving around and placing a distance between the shepherdesses and the animals. Time to get them back. Besides, it is almost time for the midday meal. With the help of the dog, the girls collect the herd and get it to follow them to the shaded area under the oak tree. The sheep and goats lie there chewing their cud while Abigail and Tamar get the food out of their pouches and spread a table. Their meal is similar to that of the men, yet somewhat different. Because they are on the move, their meal does not include oil and vinegar, and they are not able to enjoy freshly parched grain. However, their mothers packed for them handfuls of raisins and a piece of dried fig cake. Like the men, water from the skin is their drink of choice.

Since they have no place they need to rush to, they eat slowly, enjoying every bite. They would like to allow the sheep to chew their cud because this, they know, helps with the production of milk, and that is what herding is all about. Almost. The animals will have another chance at grazing on their way back home. When they are done with their meal, Tamar pours some water into Abigail's cupped hands so the dog can drink. He laps it quickly, and they repeat it three times. They collect some food scraps and feed the dog, then take out the spinning equipment once more and continue to work until it is time to get the herd up and return home.

***

After the males and the two girls leave for their appointed destinations, Hodiah and Zeruiah start their climb uphill with heavy, water-filled jars on their heads. Each has a ring made of soft material placed on her head under the jar. This helps them to balance the jar while walking erect. It takes years of training to be able to do this without the need to stabilize the jar with one's hands. They walk on the beaten path from the well to the hamlet. Before reaching the top of the hill, they reach a fork in the road; the one to the right takes them directly to their complex. They cherish this shortcut because every step counts when carrying water from the well. They repeat this four or five times before the large jars by the door are full. This depends, of course, on the amount of water consumed before the first walk to the well. Besides for drinking and watering some of the animals, they use water for cooking, washing dishes, watering the vegetable garden, and washing their faces and hands. They cannot afford to use this water for laundry; for this they will need to go down to the well. Even then, they will do it seldom and will be very careful not to waste water unnecessarily.

When the large jars are full, Zeruiah walks to the well once more and brings one more jar to water the garden. With a bowl, she measures how much water she pours next to each plant. Their garden is not different from the gardens of the other families in Ether. Between the fig, pomegranate, apricot, and carob trees lie beds of cucumbers, leeks, garlic, and watermelons. These vegetables are a special treat for the family because they are seasonal, short-lived, and cannot be processed for later consumption. When done with this chore, Zeruiah goes back into the house and gets some fodder for the oxen and the ram that are kept outside in the shed. She also feeds the calves that the family is trying to fatten. Finally, she sets up what is necessary for grinding grain, a chore she will undertake in the afternoon.

As the other women are busy bringing water from the well into the large jars by the door, Bathya finishes cleaning the house. She takes the kitchen scraps and buries them in the garden. They will turn into compost that enriches the soil. Then, while it is still cool, Bathya goes out of the hamlet into the countryside to collect field greens and roots that can be used to supplement the daily diet. She is in no rush because there is nothing urgent for her to do. This activity keeps her occupied until noon, when all those who stayed home will gather for the midday meal.

After pouring the last of the water jars from the well, Hodiah goes to the small room on the ground floor where the milk from this morning's milking was kept in a hole-mouth jar. She picks the jar up and takes it out to a shady spot outside the house. Here she has a tripod made of three long sticks tied together at the top, from which a goatskin is dangling. The leg openings are tied tightly, and the neck is open for the time being. She calls Joash to give her a hand. While he hold the skin upright, stretching the neck opening with his little hands, she pours the milk into the skin and then ties the neck opening very tight. Then she lets the skin hang horizontally from the tripod and starts shaking it like a pendulum back and forth. Joash sits beside her, ready to lend a hand whenever he will be called to. The swinging motion separates the fat from the rest of the milk and will be used for making butter. Some of the milk will be saved and mixed with the milk from the evening milking to make other products such as yogurt and cheese. While swinging the skin, Hodiah starts humming a tune that helps her drive the boredom away. Then she notices that Joash is still sitting next to her, so she starts telling him stories, some of which he has already heard before. After a while, Joash gets up and starts wandering around the open space in front of the house picking up dung, collecting it into the hem of his tunic, and taking it to the pile he has been maintaining inside next to the bread oven. He does this whenever his aunt does not ask him to relieve her from swinging the goatskin.

After he finishes straightening the ground floor, Jotham gets ready to fix some of the tools and implements that are used in the farm. Since Malkiel would like to start threshing tomorrow, Jotham plans first to attend to the implements that will be involved in this chore. He decides to tackle this task in the order in which it will be carried out. This calls for beginning with the inspection of the threshing sledge. There are several ways to thresh the crops, but the most efficient is with a sledge. The Ahuzam family owns a sledge that has been passed from one generation to another. No one knows for sure who constructed the sledge, but in spite of its age and with seasonal upkeep, the implement is indeed useable. The sledge is made of two thick, wide boards attached to each other with mortise and tenon. It has the parts necessary for hitching a pair of animals to pull it forward. On the underside, the front part is cut on a slant, something that allows the sledge to glide over the stalks without getting stuck in the ground. Furthermore, embedded in the underside are blades made mostly of flint and a few of iron. These blades separate the grain from the stalk and cut the glumes into small pieces. Jotham checks the blades to make sure that each is well secured in its place. He replaces any that are missing with a new blade, which he affixes firmly with bitumen. He also inspects the ropes by which the pulling animals will be harnessed to the sledge. When he is done with the sledge, Jotham goes on to inspect and fix the other implements, including the winnowing fork and the wooden shovel for throwing the grain in the air to separate it from the chaff. Finally, he inspects the different sieves that will be used in the final cleaning of the grain. The Ahuzam family owns a series of sieves of different sizes that help them in this task. By the time Jotham is done fixing the threshing implements, it is already time for the midday meal. Tomorrow he will attend to the plows.

It is a little past noon. The sun is at its highest position of the day, and the shadows are short. Time for the midday meal. Hodiah goes into the house to prepare the meal, but not before asking Joash to continue swinging and churning the milk. This process is almost done and should not be interrupted. Zeruiah, who has just finished taking care of the animals in the outside shed and setting up for grain grinding, comes to her aid. They bring up to the second story a pile of flat bread baked early this morning, vegetables, juglets of oil and vinegar, small bowls to be used for dipping, and a goatskin containing yogurt made yesterday. Before sitting down, Hodiah takes out a bowlfull of lentils and puts it in water to soak for the evening meal.

By now Bathya has returned from her wandering in the countryside picking field greens, which will be added to the evening meal. On her way back she passes by one of their terraced vineyards and picks two ripe grape bunches that they will share at the end of the meal. Though it is still early in the season, sometimes she can find ripe grapes ready to be eaten, especially on the southern slope.

Jotham, Bathya, Hodiah, Zeruiah, and Joash sit together on the floor in a circle a little to the south of the middle of the second story, where the light pours in through the roof opening, yet still in the shade. They eat and talk about what they accomplished up until now. Hodiah and Zeruiah share some of the gossip and news they picked up at the well this morning. When they are done, Bathya collects the bowls and other vessels to be washed on the ground floor and to be readied for the evening meal.

*　*　*

After a short nap, when the sun starts heading west and the air starts cooling down with the help of a breeze from the Great Sea, the men go back to their task of barley harvesting. They are going to continue with this task until sundown. Malkiel joins Obadiah and Zechariah on the first afternoon trip of the loaded donkeys to the threshing floor. Although the donkeys can work without being watered for the rest of the day, he would like to pass by the well and let them have a drink to reward them for their hard work. Upon their arrival at the threshing floor, Malkiel helps the boys unload the donkeys and pile up the sheaves in a neat pile at the edge of the floor. He makes sure that their pile does not get mixed with the piles belonging to the other Ether families. His task for the rest of the day until sundown is to clean the threshing floor and to get it ready for the beginning of threshing, which will start tomorrow morning. He has done it many times before and knows where to position the pile and where to conduct the winnowing so the straw and chaff will fall at the right side and will not fly in his face while the grain will drop just at the right place for sieving.

The boys return to the field. They will make one more trip and return to the threshing floor at the end of the day. On this trip they will load the donkeys to the maximum; whatever the donkeys cannot carry, they will place in a pile.

The harvesters continue with their task of reaping. They switch roles from time to time so they can maintain the pace until the end of the day. They are almost done with this plot, and by the end of the day it will be finished. They look forward to that because they would like to start with the wheat harvest the next day.

It is getting cooler as the sun migrates west, and the field is getting darker because of the long shadows of the hills on its western side. The harvesters finish reaping the whole field with the exception of a corner, which they leave standing for the gleaners and the other needy poor. As the sun goes down rapidly, they collect all the sheaves into a neat pile from which they load the donkeys for the last trip to the threshing floor and home. They would like to finish this task before it is completely dark because they do not want to leave any of the sheaves behind. In such a case, the sheaf cannot be retrieved the next day and becomes the property of the needy. They also would like to travel home while they can still see the way. They are quite familiar with the path that was cleared from stones by them and others. The path reflects the moonlight and is quite visible, but they would rather not delay too long in the field.

As the girls sit under the oak tree, the sun moves and the sheep and goats change position in order to avoid the sunlight. The animals lie on the ground with their eyes closed as if in deep sleep. The only telling sign that they are not asleep is the continuous chewing of their cud, which, in addition to their split hoof, is a mark that these animals can be consumed as food and offered as sacrifice. The animals lie in a circle, and when an individual animal is bathed in sunlight, it gets up and goes to the other side of the circle to be in the shade. This continuous motion keeps the herd awake and chewing.

The sun continues to move, and eventually they completely lose their shade. It is time to get up and prepare to go home. The trip back home takes time because the animals continue to graze as they walk. Their noses are kept so close to the ground that it looks as if they lick the dirt. Indeed, in some spots hardly any pasture is visible, but the animals find something to chomp on.

Abigail, who walks at the head of the herd, pulls out her flute once more and plays a tune, while Tamar stays behind the flock and with the help of the dog exerts some pressure on the straggling animals to keep pace with the rest. She whistles at them, throws small stones, and yells to keep them together. The girls would like to get to the well before many of the other shepherds come. This time they are not going to have their mothers' help in watering the flock. The animals know, too, that they are going to be watered, and this keeps them going in the right direction.

They arrive at the well when two other herds are already there. Luckily, since they belong to village families, all the herds are relatively small. It will not be too long before their turn comes. In the meantime, the shepherds exchange more of the same gossip and news. Since nothing in particular happened this day, there is no new information to exchange. Sometimes a shepherd runs into a carnivorous animal such as a wolf or a bear and needs to protect the animals. This makes for a good and exciting story that is rehearsed and gets embellished as time goes on. But today was just a typical hot summer day.

When their turn comes, Abigail and Tamar draw water from the deep well with a long goat-hair rope attached to a wide-mouth jar. They pour the water into the stone troughs and let the animals drink as much as they want. Now it is time to get on the path uphill to the hamlet. The animals do not hesitate because they know that upon their return they will get some fodder. This is a good way to entice the sheep and goats to return home.

***

After the midday meal, Jotham joins two other men of his age from the Palti and Shimi families, and they go down the slope to one of the cisterns, where they intend to continue the task they started a few days earlier of cleaning the cistern in anticipation of the rainy season. This is a cooperative effort because it takes several people to tackle it. Besides, the cisterns are shared by all who live at Ether. Two of them climb down the wooden ladder, and one of them, with the help of a metal hoe, fills a straw basket with the silt that accumulated at the bottom of the cistern during the last winter. The other one carries it up the ladder and hands it to the third man, who stayed outside. He takes the silt and dumps it down hill. The silt can be used in the future to fertilize the gardens and the trees near the house. As with other projects, the men change roles from time to time so they will not get exhausted. They work like this for a few hours until just before dusk. They stop work in time to go to a nearby cistern, where they catch a few pigeons just returning for their nighttime sleep.

Bathya, who spent the morning outside, prefers to spend the afternoon in the house or just next to it. Every afternoon she engages in weaving. Her upright loom is set on the ground floor in a small room near where the fodder is kept. This is a good location because she can participate in the conversation that is carried on by all the women who are busy there with different tasks. She has been working on this particular piece of cloth for two days and is almost done. She will probably finish it by the time everyone is back from his or her outdoors chores. The loom is made of two upright wooden beams leaning against the wall, with their bottoms each set in a round stone hollowed in the middle. This keeps them from sliding. At their tops, the uprights are connected to each other with a horizontal wooden beam. The vertical strings, the warp, are tied to this horizontal beam, and their bottom ends are each tied to a clay weight that is circular with a hole in the middle. Bathya has a large collection of weights of different sizes that she keeps in a circular bin. The different weights enable her to weave different kinds of cloth. For the weft, as well as for the warp, she uses wool yarn that was spun by her and by the other females of the family whenever they had time. She weaves patterns with yarn she dyed with pigments from different sources, plants and minerals. She uses bone spatulas to perform pattern weaving. The different balls of yarn are kept within her reach in open bowls with holes in their bottoms. Bathya runs the yarn through the hole while the ball is kept inside the bowl. This prevents the balls from rolling on the ground and helps her maintain their cleanliness.

Zeruiah, who before the midday meal prepared her flour-grinding station, is busily engaged carrying out her intended task. Earlier she brought from the storage room in a large bowl a measure of wheat that will suffice for two days. She wants to grind enough flour for two days because tomorrow afternoon she intends to be busy making cheese, some of which she intends to turn into dry cheese. Grinding is done by placing some grain on top of a large, concave stone. For that, Zeruiah uses a large hunk of smooth flint. She kneels while she rubs the grain with a smaller, elongated piece of flint, which she holds with her hands at both ends. She rubs the stones one against the other, back and forth, with the grain in between until it turns to flour. When she is satisfied with the result, she collects the flour with her bare hands and puts it inside a hole-mouth jar. Flour can be kept this way for about three days. She repeats the activity, putting grain on the lower stone and rubbing it with the upper stone. This chore is monotonous and takes quite a while, especially since Zeruiah would like to have enough flour for two days. The monotony leads her to start humming a tune that is recognized by the other women, who join in.

Hodiah's responsibility is to get the evening meal together. She has plenty of time to cook something delicious. Tonight it is vegetarian stew. She asks Joash to bring some dung for fuel and some cracked olive pits from last year's pressing for kindling. She starts the fire in the hearth with a piece of coal left burning in the bread oven. While Joash keeps an eye on the fire, she goes to the vegetable garden and digs up a few carrots and picks a medium-sized gourd and a large cucumber. Hodiah washes them in one of the large bowls she has stacked on the ground floor by the water jars. Later she sends Joash to pour the water in the garden. She fills up a large-mouth cooking pot halfway with water and puts it in the middle of the fire. Joash remains in charge of stocking the fire. In the meantime, Hodiah puts aside the cucumber and cuts the other cleaned vegetables into small pieces so they can cook faster. When the water is boiling, she puts the cut carrots and gourd in the pot and adds the lentils she started soaking before sitting down for the midday meal. She goes into the storage room and takes off the shelf a block of salt that Shmaryahu bought in the market last time he went there. She takes the rock to her stone workbench and with a rounded hammer-stone breaks off a piece, which she drops into the pot. Then she takes some ground cumin from one small bowl and about the same amount of dill weed from another, then drops the herbs into the pot. By that time the whole mixture in the pot is boiling. She mixes it all with a smooth stick and tastes it with her tongue. She needs to adjust the taste until she is satisfied. Now that the stew is cooking, she hands the stick to Joash and instructs him to mix it every few minutes. Throughout this process, Hodiah can hear the other women humming and singing in a low voice, so, whenever she does not need to concentrate, she joins them.

Zeruiah continues to grind enough flour for two days because tomorrow she wants to use the afternoon for making cheese. She is almost done but is interrupted by Hodiah, who asks her to take some of the wheat and mash it for the stew. Zeruiah takes two handfuls of wheat, puts it in a stone mortar that has been resting near the grinding station, and mashes the grain to bits with a stone pestle. She picks up the mortar and brings it next to the hearth, where Hodiah scoops the mashed grain and throws it into the pot, while Zeruiah gets back to her grinding. Hodiah mixes everything well in the pot and covers it with a slab of limestone, then returns to her workbench, where she left the cucumber. She takes another medium-sized bowl and fills it halfway with some curds from the morning churning. Tomorrow Zeruiah will use the rest of it in her cheese making. She takes the cucumber and cuts it into small pieces right into the bowl. The pieces are so small they seem to be grated. She takes two cloves of dry garlic that is hanging from the rafters, peels them, mashes them finely, and puts them in the bowl. She picks up some of the salt that remained on the bench from her previous encounter with the rock salt and puts it in the bowl together with a pinch of cumin. When this concoction is all well mixed, it is ready for dipping bread.

By this time the stew is ready. Hodiah moves it to the edge of the hearth and gets another cooking pot filled with water. She tells Joash to keep the fire going because, after placing the pot in the middle of the hearth, she wants to boil water in anticipation for the possibility of having Jotham bring pigeons for the evening meal.

***

Indeed, Jotham is first to arrive. He and his cohorts were successful in catching a few pigeons. Each got two. After pulling off the feathers, he cleaned the pigeons with a sharp knife that is usually tucked in his leather belt. By the time he gets home, the water in the second cooking pot is boiling. Hodiah cuts the pigeons into several pieces that can fit into the pot and drops them in to boil.

A familiar bark can be heard from the outside. Abigail and Tamar are back. They herd the sheep and goats into the stalls next to the room with the fodder, then bring some feed made of barley mixed with chopped straw and put it in the wooden troughs. The animals were expecting it and start nudging each other for a place at the trough, into which they stick their faces right away. While munching on the feed, they are being milked for the second time of the day. Abigail is doing the honors, while Jotham and Tamar keep the animals from moving or kicking in frustration. When the milking is over, the ewes are united with the lambs and kids for a short session of nursing, after which they are separated again and the young ones are led to their side of the stalls, where another helping of mashed grain mixed in some milk is awaiting them. While all this is taking place, Shmaryahu, Malkiel, Obadiah, and Zechariah return. Malkiel met them at the threshing floor when they arrived with the final load of the day and showed them where to unload. Together they made their way to the house. They come into the house accompanied by the two donkeys, which are taken into their side room, tied with a rope that is placed through a hole in the stone trough, and given fodder and water.

***

Everyone is back in the house. Time for the evening meal. They wash hands and faces, trying to conserve some of the water to be used the next day in watering the garden and the animals. The meal will take place in the center of the second floor under the opening through which they can gaze at the stars. The moon is waning, but the sky is clear and enough light streams in. Nevertheless, Jotham brings up a few oil lamps, which he lights with a branch he snatched from the fire downstairs. Then he places the lamps in choice locations to get their maximum light. Bathya brings up a stack of individual bowls and the washed greens she collected earlier. The Ahuzam family is well to do and can afford having an individual bowl for each family member. Tamar carries a stack of flat bread to the second floor, and Abigail brings some of the fresh milk just obtained. This will give them some change from the water they have been drinking all day long. After dropping the boiled pigeons into the stew, Hodiah proudly and carefully passes it to Jotham. Zeruiah nimbly climbs up the ladder with the yogurt dip in one hand. The others join the family circle, all taking the spots they regularly occupy whenever they assemble for a communal meal. With the help of a scoop made of a broken lamp, Hodiah pours a measure of stew into each bowl, and the bowls are passed around. The stack of bread is also passed around, and they all serve themselves. They dip bread in the yogurt bowl and gulp the stew straight from the bowl. Using the bread, they push cooked pieces into their mouth. The milk bowl is passed around for everyone to have a mouthful or two. The same is done with the water skin. They have seconds, and after finishing, each one wipes the inside of the bowl with a piece of bread and turns the bowl upside down to indicate completion of the meal. Not much is said during the meal except for requests for passing this or that.

When the meal is over, it is time to talk about the day's events. They rehash what they have done and begin to coordinate tomorrow's activities. Abigail is eager to show her grandfather how well she can play the song he taught her two days earlier. Tomorrow is another big day, and they need to start it early. They do not have time to sit around and chat. Bathya still needs to wash the bowls, and she does so with help by Zeruiah, who also helps her by carrying down two of the lamps. Tamar and Abigail take a final look at the herd animals to make sure that all is well. They also take care of the dog that will be with them again tomorrow by giving him some pigeon bones, table scraps, and water. Hodiah makes sure the fire in the hearth is out and places one oil lamp to keep the ladder lit. Before retiring to the roof, every individual goes out of the compound in a given direction to take care of private needs. With no facilities available, they do it in the open under the cover of darkness. The same problem exists during daytime, and they need to take care of it individually.

At this point, they are all ready to go to bed. They will sleep again on the roof, where it is cool and pleasant.

And it was evening and it was morning, one day in the life of the Ahuzam family.

NOTES

PREFACE

[1] The interest in daily life has recently increased. Before the completion of this book, a new and attractive work was published by two leading scholars; see Philip J. King and Lawrence E. Stager, *Life in Biblical Israel* (Library of Ancient Israel; Louisville: Westminster John Knox, 2001).

[2] Oded Borowski, *Agriculture in Iron Age Israel* (Winona Lake, Ind.: Eisenbrauns, 1987; repr., Boston: American Schools of Oriental Research, 2002); Oded Borowski, *Every Living Thing: Daily Use of Animals in Ancient Israel* (Walnut Creek, Calif.: AltaMira, 1998).

CHAPTER 1

[1] Amihai Mazar, *Archaeology of the Land of the Bible: 10,000–586 B.C.E.* (New York: Doubleday, 1990), 1.

[2] This term is used here in reference to the area settled by the Israelites and other ethnic groups on both sides of the Jordan during long stretches of the Iron Age (ca. 1200–586 B.C.E.). Before the Israelite settlement, this area is known in biblical terminology as Canaan. It was known to the neighboring peoples by other names.

[3] The borders of the land settled by the Israelites fluctuated and changed from time to time. At times, the Israelites controlled parts of Transjordan, and at times they considered their land to stretch "from Dan to Beer-sheba" (Judg 20:1). The land of Judah was mainly "from Geba to Beer-sheba" (2 Kgs 23:8). What is discussed here is not the political but geographical limits.

[4] For more on the Sea Peoples and the Philistines, see Trude Dothan, *The Philistines and Their Material Culture* (Jerusalem: Israel Exploration Society, 1982); Trude Dothan and Moshe Dothan, *People of the Sea: The Search for the Philistines* (New York: Macmillan, 1992); for the Sikils, see Ephraim Stern, *Dor, The Ruler of the Seas: Nineteen Years of Excavations at the Israelite-Phoenician Harbor Town on the Carmel Coast* (Jerusalem: Israel Exploration Society, 2000); for the Shardanu, see Adam Zertal, "Philistine Kin Found in Early Israel," *BAR* 28/3 (2002): 18–31, 60–61; for the Phoenicians, see Françoise Briquel-Chatonnet, *Les relations entre les cités de la côte phénicienne et les royaumes d'Israël et de Juda* (OLA 46; Leuven: Departement Oriëntalistiek, Peeters, 1992); Françoise Briquel-Chatonnet and E. Gubel, *Les Phéniciens: Aux origines du Liban* (Paris: Gallimard, 1998); Eric Gubel, *Les Phéniciens et le monde méditerranéen* (Brussels: Generale Bank [Belgium]/Banque générale du Luxembourg, 1986); Eric Gubel and Edward Lipiński, eds., *Phoenicia and Its Neighbours: Proceedings of the Colloquium Held on the 9th and 10th of December 1983 at the "Vrije Universiteit Brussel," in Cooperation with the "Centrum Voor Myceense En Archaïsch-Griekse Cultuur"* (Studia Phoenicia 3; Leuven: Peeters, 1985).

[5] See Yohanan Aharoni and Michael Avi-Yonah, *The Macmillan Bible Atlas* (New York: Macmillan, 1968), 9, 10; Barry J. Beitzel, *The Moody Atlas of Bible Lands* (Chicago: Moody Press, 1985), maps 18–19.

[6] It is hard to say what a normal year is, since there are so many droughts caused either by an overall lack of precipitation or bad timing.

[7] Space prohibits dealing with this very complicated question in more than a brief way. For more on this question, see, e.g., William G. Dever, "Archaeology, Ideology, and the Quest for 'Ancient' or 'Biblical' Israel," *Near Eastern Archaeology* 61/1 (1998): 39–52; William G. Dever, *What Did the Biblical Writers Know and When Did They Know It?* (Grand Rapids: Eerdmans, 2001); Israel Finkelstein, "Ethnicity and Origin of the Iron I Settlers in the Highlands of Canaan: Can the Real Israel Stand Up?" *BA* 59 (1996): 198–212; and the bibliographies there.

[8] Not all of these groups can be identified.

[9] Some call it "proto-Israelite." At this point it is not important whether this entity was a new ethnic or a particular socioeconomic group of an already-established group. What is important here is the fact that the highlands of Canaan became occupied by a new entity that can be distinguished from older ones. Later it developed into what is considered monarchic Israel.

[10] See, e.g., Ezek 16:3, 45.

[11] Finkelstein, "Ethnicity and Origin," 209.

[12] Frank J. Yurco, "Merneptah's Canaanite Campaign and Israel's Origins," in *Exodus: The Egyptian Evidence* (ed. E. S. Frerichs and L. H. Lesko; Winona Lake, Ind.: Eisenbrauns, 1997).

[13] *ANET,* fig 100a.

[14] David Ussishkin, *The Conquest of Lachish by Sennacherib* (Tel Aviv: Institute of Archaeology, Tel Aviv University, 1982).

[15] Estimating the population of early periods such as the Iron Age is difficult because of the different factors that have to be considered and their inaccuracy. Two of these factors are the area actually settled and population density, neither of which can be accurately measured. For bibliography concerning past studies and methodologies, see Magen Broshi, "Methodology of Population Estimates: The Roman-Byzantine Period As a Case Study," in *Biblical Archaeology Today, 1990: Proceedings of the Second International Congress on Biblical Archaeology* (ed. A. Biran and J. Aviram; Jerusalem: Israel Exploration Society; Israel Academy of Sciences and Humanities, 1993); Yigal Shiloh, "The Population of Iron Age Palestine in the Light of a Sample Analysis of Urban Plans, Areas, and Population Density," *BASOR* 239 (1980): 23–35.

[16] Israel Finkelstein, *The Archaeology of the Israelite Settlement* (trans. D. Saltz; Jerusalem: Israel Exploration Society, 1988), 330–56. In a later publication, Finkelstein estimates the population at the end of Iron Age I in the area of "Israelite settlement" at ca. 65,000, while the total population of western Palestine around 1000 B.C.E. would have reached ca. 150,000 (Israel Finkelstein, "Environmental Archaeology and Social History: Demographic and Economic Aspects of the Monarchic Period," in *Biblical Archaeology Today, 1990: Proceedings of the Second International Congress on Biblical Archaeology* [ed. A. Biran and J. Aviram; Jerusalem: Israel Exploration Society; Israel Academy of Sciences and Humanities, 1993], 60). Broshi estimates that around 1200 B.C.E. the population was about 60,000; see Broshi, "Methodology of Population Estimates," 423 n. 2.

[17] Finkelstein, "Environmental Archaeology," 58.

[18] Magen Broshi and Israel Finkelstein, "The Population of Palestine in Iron Age II," *BASOR* 287 (1992): 47–60; Finkelstein, "Environmental Archaeology."

[19] Finkelstein, "Environmental Archaeology," 59.

[20] Ibid.

CHAPTER 2

[1] Ze'ev Herzog, *Archaeology of the City: Urban Planning in Ancient Israel and Its Social Implications* (Tel Aviv: Institute of Archaeology, Tel Aviv University, 1997), 276.

[2] Finkelstein, "Environmental Archaeology," 62.

[3] Herzog, *Archaeology of the City,* 276.

[4] On cutting trees and building terraces, see Borowski, *Agriculture in Iron Age Israel*, 15–20. On the difficulties in securing land for cultivation, see Carol Meyers, "The Family in Ancient Israel," in *Families in Ancient Israel: The Family, Religion, and Culture* (Louisville: Westminster John Knox, 1997), 3.

[5] The same is true with selection of cemetery sites.

[6] Lawrence E. Stager, "The Archaeology of the Family in Ancient Israel," *BASOR* 260 (1985): 3, fig. 1 and table 1.

[7] The NRSV translates "her daughters" as "its villages."

[8] Volkmar Fritz, *The City in Ancient Israel* (Sheffield: Sheffield Academic Press, 1995), 68.

[9] However, Fritz disagrees with the interpretation of certain sites as cult-related; see his arguments contra A. Mazar on the bull site (*The City in Ancient Israel*, 70 n. 24); Zertal on the Mount Ebal site (70 n. 23); and Yassin on Tell el-Mazar (70 n. 24).

[10] Ibid., 68. For examples of such villages, see Herzog, *Archaeology of the City*, 149 and fig. 17.

[11] Fritz, *The City in Ancient Israel*, 69–70.

[12] Ram Gophna, "Iron Age I Ḥāṣērîm in Southern Philistia," *Atiqot* (Hebrew Series) 3 (1966): 41–51, *5–*6.

[13] On the four-room house, see below. Fritz suggests that the ring shape "corresponds to the shape of the Bedouin camp, in which tents are grouped around an open area. Apart from the defensive function, this shape is determined by the common use of the area enclosed … a place of shelter for animals" (*The City in Ancient Israel*, 69). This suggestion follows Finkelstein's in *The Archaeology of the Israelite Settlement* (244–50) but cannot be supported because this form of encampment is reserved by the bedouin only for special occasions, such as wedding celebrations. Furthermore, in discussing the origins of the four-room house, Fritz rejects the notion that it has nomadic origins (*The City in Ancient Israel*, 74–75).

[14] Fritz, *The City in Ancient Israel*, 69.

[15] For details on these sites, see ibid.

[16] Examples of farmsteads during the Iron Age II are the so-called fortresses in the Negev and the settlements in the Buqeiʾah (east of the Dead Sea). See also Shimon Dar, "The Relationship between the Dwelling Place and the Family in Ancient Israel," *ErIsr* 25 (1996): 154.

[17] This term is used for both the physical and social entities; see, e.g., ibid., 151–52. For more on the family, see below.

[18] Fritz suggests that before the development of the three- and four-room house there was another type that he names the pillar-house, which had its origins in the Canaanite house and later evolved in the highlands settlements into the four-room house. As examples he cites houses at ʿIzbet Ṣarṭah Stratum II and Ḥorvat Masos Stratum II. This house type is distinguished by being divided lengthwise by two rows of pillars into three units. According to Fritz, the middle space was not roofed over because of its width and probably served as a courtyard (*The City in Ancient Israel*, 73–74). Because of several common characteristics, such as the stone pillars and long rooms, there is no reason to see this as a distinct house type, and it should be considered one of the four-room-house variants (similarly to the tripartite storehouse), probably an early one. Furthermore, if Fritz is right in assuming that the pillar-house was borrowed from the Canaanite sedentary culture, there is no good reason to assume that the ring-shaped village evolved from the bedouin encampment.

[19] Yigal Shiloh, "The Four-Room House—the Israelite Type-House," *ErIsr* 11 (1973): 277–85; Yigal Shiloh, "The Four-Room House: Its Situation and Function in the Israelite City," *IEJ* 20 (1970): 180–90.

[20] In an early study, Shiloh reached the conclusion that the four-room house was exclusively Israelite (Shiloh, "The Four-Room House—the Israelite Type-House"). However, further research points out that this house type cannot be identified with a particular ethnic group.

21 Ehud Netzer, "Domestic Architecture in the Iron Age," in *The Architecture of Ancient Israel: From the Prehistoric to the Persian Periods* (ed. A. Kempinski and R. Reich; Jerusalem: Israel Exploration Society, 1991), 193; Fritz, *The City in Ancient Israel,* 73.

22 Fritz, *The City in Ancient Israel,* 73–74.

23 Netzer, "Domestic Architecture in the Iron Age," 196 fig. 6, 197 fig. 7.

24 Lily Singer-Avitz, "Household Activities at Beersheba," *ErIsr* 25 (1996): 169–70.

25 Netzer, "Domestic Architecture in the Iron Age," 198; Singer-Avitz, "Household Activities at Beersheba," 170. Where large pillars were not available, smaller stone sections (drums) were placed one on top of the other.

26 Netzer, "Domestic Architecture in the Iron Age," 198.

27 Palaces also had second stories (2 Kgs 1:2). See more below.

28 This description is based on the Greek translation.

29 Compare this to Mark Twain's experience of staying in an Arab village: "We could have slept in the largest of the houses, but there were some little drawbacks; it was populous with vermin, it had a dirt floor, it was in no respect cleanly, and there was a family of goats in the only bedroom, and two donkeys in the parlor" (Daniel Morley McKeithan, ed., *Traveling with the Innocents Abroad: Mark Twain's Original Reports from Europe and the Holy Land* [Norman: University of Oklahoma Press, 1958], 263). On the use of space in the Iron Age house, see James W. Hardin, "An Archaeology of Destruction: Households and the Use of Domestic Space at Iron II Tel Halif" (Ph.D. diss., University of Arizona, 2001).

30 Singer-Avitz, "Household Activities at Beersheba," 170.

31 Shiloh, "The Four-Room House—the Israelite Type-House," 280.

32 Netzer, "Domestic Architecture in the Iron Age," 199.

33 Ibid., 197–99.

34 Singer-Avitz, "Household Activities at Beersheba," 166, 171–71.

35 Dar, "Relationship between the Dwelling Place and the Family," 153.

36 Division into stories and different rooms could have been for purity (Netzer, "Domestic Architecture in the Iron Age," 199).

37 It should be pointed out that the father was usually the spokesman of the family in legal matters (Deut 22:16).

38 For more on the family, see below.

39 For more on the elders, see Victor H. Matthews and Don C. Benjamin, *Social World of Ancient Israel 1250–587 BCE* (Peabody, Mass.: Hendrickson, 1993); Hanoch Reviv, *The Elders in Ancient Israel* (trans. L. Plitmann; Jerusalem: Magnes; Hebrew University, 1989).

40 For more details on the family in biblical times, see Joseph Blenkinsopp, "The Family in First Temple Israel," in *The Family, Religion, and Culture* (Louisville: Westminster John Knox, 1997); Meyers, "The Family in Ancient Israel"; J. David Schloen, *The House of the Father As Fact and Symbol: Patrimonialism in Ugarit and the Ancient Near East* (ed. L. E. Stager; Studies in the Archaeology and History of the Levant; Winina Lake, Ind.: Eisenbrauns, 2001).

41 Meyers, "The Family in Ancient Israel," 13.

42 Blenkinsopp, "The Family in First Temple Israel," 57.

43 Meyers, "The Family in Ancient Israel," 25, 35.

44 Oded Borowski, "Hezekiah's Reforms and the Revolt against Assyria," *BA* 58 (1995): 148–55.

45 For a detailed discussion of Israelite religion, see Ziony Zevit, *The Religions of Ancient Israel: A Synthesis of Parallactic Approaches* (New York: Continuum, 2001).

46 On the agricultural calendar and its relationship to the cult, see below.

47 Actually, the legal system was designed for the same purpose.

48 Blenkinsopp, "The Family in First Temple Israel," 53.

49 See above, ch. 1.

50 Meyers, "The Family in Ancient Israel," 3.

[51] Obviously, the length of day changed with the seasons.

[52] Blenkinsopp, "The Family in First Temple Israel," 54–56.

[53] See above, ch. 1.

[54] As in Borowski, *Agriculture in Iron Age Israel,* 38.

[55] For details, see ibid., 31–44.

[56] For details on wine and oil making, see Rafael Frankel, *Ancient Olive Pressing Installations* [Hebrew] (Tel Aviv: Ha'aretz Museum, 1986); Rafael Frankel, Shmuel Avitsur, and Etan Ayalon, *History and Technology of Olive Oil in the Holy Land* (trans. J. C. Jacobson; Arlington, Va.: Oléarius Editions; Tel Aviv: Eretz Israel Museum, 1994); Carey Ellen Walsh, *The Fruit of the Vine: Viticulture in Ancient Israel and the Hebrew Bible* (HSM 60; Winona Lake, Ind.: Eisenbrauns, 2000).

[57] On herding, see Borowski, *Every Living Thing.*

[58] On pottery making and its distribution in ancient Palestine, see Bryant G. Wood, *The Sociology of Pottery in Ancient Palestine: The Ceramic Industry and the Diffusion of Ceramic Style in the Bronze and Iron Ages* (JSOTSup 103; Sheffield: JSOT Press, 1990).

[59] The most common loom weights found at Israelite sites are donut-shaped. On loom weights and weaving, see Glenda Friend, *Tell Taannek 1963–1968 III/2: The Loom Weights* (ed. K. Nashef; Birzeit: Palestinian Institute of Archaeology, Birzeit University, 1998).

[60] Borowski, *Agriculture in Iron Age Israel,* 98–99.

[61] Avraham Biran, *Biblical Dan* (Jerusalem: Israel Exploration Society and Hebrew Union College-Jewish Institute of Religion, 1994), 147–57.

[62] Mazar, *Archaeology of the Land of the Bible,* 350–51.

[63] For wars in biblical times, see Jacob Liver, ed., *The Military History of the Land of Israel in Biblical Times* [Hebrew] (Military Historical Library; Tel Aviv: Maarachot, 1964); Yigael Yadin, *The Art of Warfare in Biblical Lands in the Light of Archaeological Study* (New York: McGraw-Hill, 1963).

[64] Recorded sea battles in general are limited. One of them is that of the Sea Peoples against Ramesses III (ca. 1175 B.C.E.).

[65] On the ideology of war, see Gerhard von Rad, *Holy War in Ancient Israel* (trans. and ed. M. J. Dawn; Grand Rapids: Eerdmans, 1991).

[66] *ANET,* 320.

[67] Much of what is described below was not invented by the Israelites and is known to have been in use by other armies, such as the Egyptians and the Hittites.

[68] On the question of the drinking test by Gideon, see Abraham Malamat, "Gideon's War against Midian," in *The Military History of the Land of Israel in Biblical Times* [Hebrew] (ed. J. Liver; Tel Aviv: Maarachot, 1964).

[69] James C. Vanderkam, "Prophecy and Apocalyptics in the Ancient Near East," *CANE,* 2085.

[70] Priestly paraphernalia used for predicting the future.

[71] Recently Adam Zertal ("Philistine Kin Found in Early Israel") has suggested that Sisera was a Shardanu who cooperated with the Canaanites.

[72] Attacking from different directions was not limited to the Israelites. According to biblical accounts, the Philistines also used the tactic of attacking from more than one direction (1 Sam 13:17).

CHAPTER 3

[1] See, e.g., Fritz, *The City in Ancient Israel;* Herzog, *Archaeology of the City;* Yigal Shiloh, "Elements in the Development of Town Planning in the Israelite City," *IEJ* 28(1978): 36–51; George R. H. Wright, *Ancient Building in South Syria and Palestine* (2 vols.; Leiden: Brill, 1985).

[2] Herzog, *Archaeology of the City,* 259.

[3] For more on the history of, reasons for, and theories on the rise of the city, see ibid., 259–78.

[4] Ibid., 276.

[5] Shiloh, "Elements in the Development of Town Planning."

[6] On the hierarchy of cities in the Israelite period, see Herzog, *Archaeology of the City,* 259–78; Herzog, "Settlement and Fortification Planning in the Iron Age."

[7] On fortifications in the Iron Age, see Herzog, "Settlement and Fortification Planning in the Iron Age."

[8] Ussishkin, *The Conquest of Lachish by Sennacherib.*

[9] Biran, *Biblical Dan,* 245.

[10] See Ze'ev Herzog, "The Architecture of the Israelite Fortresses in the Negev," in *The Architecture of Ancient Israel from the Prehistoric to the Persian Periods* (ed. A. Kempinski and R. Reich; Jerusalem: Israel Exploration Society, 1992).

[11] Although the physical conditions did not change in a major way, sometimes other factors, such as political changes and better understanding of the resources, caused changes to be made in existing systems or construction of a sister system, as in Megiddo, Jerusalem, and Gibeon.

[12] Yigal Shiloh, "Underground Water Systems in the Land of Israel in the Iron Age," in *The Architecture of Ancient Israel from the Prehistoric to the Persian Periods* (ed. A. Kempinski and R. Reich; Jerusalem: Israel Exploration Society, 1992).

[13] Until the recent excavations by Reich and Shukron, the Warren Shaft in Jerusalem was considered as belonging to this group; see Hershel Shanks, "Everything You Ever Knew about Jerusalem Is Wrong (Well, Almost)," *BAR* 25/6 (1999); Hershel Shanks, "I Climbed Warren's Shaft (but Joab Never Did)," *BAR* 25/6 (1999).

[14] In the latter three, the systems collected runoff water.

[15] Wright, *Ancient Building in South Syria and Palestine,* 59–60.

[16] Ronny Reich, "Palaces and Residences in the Iron Age," in *The Architecture of Ancient Israel from the Prehistoric to the Persian Periods* (ed. A. Kempinski and R. Reich; Jerusalem: Israel Exploration Society, 1992), 202.

[17] Wright, *Ancient Building in South Syria and Palestine,* 61–62.

[18] Reich, "Palaces and Residences in the Iron Age," 212.

[19] Yigal Shiloh, *The Proto-Aeolic Capital and Israelite Ashlar Masonry* (Qedem 11; Jerusalem: Hebrew University, 1979).

[20] Space does not allow here a discussion concerning the possibility that all or some of these structures were used as stables (e.g., in Megiddo) or for other purposes.

[21] For more on storage, see Borowski, *Agriculture in Iron Age Israel,* 71–83.

[22] Presently there is no information available concerning the kind of government that was in place in the northern kingdom. Inscriptional evidence suggests that, at least in part, the northern kingdom had offices similar to several of those known from the southern kingdom.

[23] On the elders in the city, see Reviv, *The Elders in Ancient Israel,* 51–75, 97–101. On the elders in general, see Matthews and Benjamin, *Social World of Ancient Israel 1250–587 BCE,* 121–31.

[24] According to Ziony Zevit (*The Religions of Ancient Israel,* 225) there were at least seventeen temples in ancient Israel.

[25] Borowski, "Hezekiah's Reforms and the Revolt against Assyria."

[26] Biran, *Biblical Dan,* 159–233.

[27] In addition to materials, barter or trading was done also in services.

[28] On the use of the horse in daily life, see Borowski, *Every Living Thing,* 99–108.

[29] For details on the Israelite weight system, see Shalom M. Paul and William G. Dever, eds., *Biblical Archaeology* (Library of Jewish Knowledge; New York: Quadrangle, 1974),

168–83; on the weight system of Judah, see Yigal Ronen, "The Enigma of the Shekel Weights of the Judean Kingdom," *BA* 59 (1996): 122–25.

[30] Ronen, "The Enigma of the Shekel Weights."

[31] Biran, *Biblical Dan;* Brian Hesse and Paula Wapnish, "Pigs' Feet, Cattle Bones and Birds' Wings," *BAR* 22/1 (1996): 62.

[32] On the domestication of the camel, see Borowski, *Every Living Thing,* 112–16.

[33] Paula Wapnish, "Beauty and Utility in Bone—New Light on Bone Crafting," in *Ashkelon Discovered: From Canaanites and Philistines to Romans and Moslems* (Washington, D.C.: Biblical Archaeology Society, 1991), 58–61.

[34] The book of Jonah is descriptive of ancient seafaring.

[35] Yigael Yadin, "'Let the Young Men Come Forward and Have a Single Combat before Us'" in *The Military History of the Land of Israel in Biblical Times* [Hebrew] (ed. J. Liver; Tel Aviv: Maarachot, 1964), 166–69.

[36] Until recent excavations in the water system, the *ṣinnôr* was identified with Warren's Shaft. It has been shown that Warren's Shaft was not available in David's time.

[37] Several scholars have maintained that the six-chambered gates and related casemate fortifications discovered at Hazor, Megiddo, and Gezer are the products of Solomon's wave of construction. A few archaeologists who would like to date it to a somewhat later period, possibly Ahab's, have challenged this recently. On the question of the Solomonic gates, see Dever, *What Did the Biblical Writers Know,* 131–38.

[38] *ANET,* 320.

[39] Ibid., 279.

CHAPTER 4

[1] See the depiction of the queen of Punt in the temple of Hatshepsut at Deir el Dahari in Kazimierz Michalowski, *Art of Ancient Egypt* (New York: Abrams, 1968), fig 92. Biblical references concerning obesity refer to Eglon king of Moab as one who "was a very fat man" (Judg 3:17), and the upper-class women of Samaria are referred to by Amos as "Bashan cows" (4:1). Being heavy of jowl and having the sides bulge with fat (Job 15:27) seems to have been a characteristic of the privileged class, as can be surmised from the utterance attributed to Moses: "Jacob ate and was well fed; Jeshurun grew fat and bloated and sleek" (Deut 32:15).

[2] Don R. Brothwell and Patricia Brothwell, *Food in Antiquity: A Survey of the Diet of Early People* (New York: Praeger, 1969), 73. The same idea is expressed by the statement "eating curds and honey" (Isa 7:15, 22).

[3] For a treatment of sacrificial animals, see, e.g., Borowski, *Every Living Thing,* 214–15.

[4] Finkelstein, "Ethnicity and Origin," 206.

[5] Adherence to these dietary laws can be measured to a certain degree by zooarchaeological evidence, and the case of the pig can serve as an example. As stated by Finkelstein, "the taboo on this animal [pig] was already practiced in the hill country in Iron I—pigs were not present in proto-Israelite Iron I sites in the highlands, while they were quite popular at a proto-Ammonite site and numerous at Philistine sites" ("Ethnicity and Origin," 206).

[6] For the question of the chicken in ancient Israel, see Borowski, *Every Living Thing,* 157–58.

[7] One *kor* = 6.25 U.S. bushels.

[8] Similar information is reported in connection with Hezekiah's temple consecration (2 Chr 29:31–35) and Hezekiah's Passover celebration (2 Chr 30:23–24).

[9] *ANET,* 560. The menu included huge amounts of cattle, calves, sheep, lambs, stags, gazelles, ducks, gees, doves, fish, jerboa, eggs, bread, wine, beer, vegetables, oils, condiments, parched barley, fruit, nuts, garlic, onions, turnips, and much more.

[10] No details are given concerning the way the calf was prepared. However, when Gideon fed a messenger, he probably boiled the young goat, since part of the meal was broth.

[11] *ANET,* 20.

[12] Avitsur suggests that the term *ḥōmeṣ* is yogurt (Shmuel Avitsur, *Man and His Work: Historical Atlas of Tools and Workshops in the Holy Land* [Jerusalem: Carta and Israel Exploration Society, 1976], 64).

[13] Middle Eastern mixture of wild thyme, salt, and summer savory.

[14] Frankel, Avitsur, and Ayalon, *History and Technology of Olive Oil,* 92.

[15] Bill Grantham, "Dinner in Buqata: The Symbolic Nature of Food Animals and Meal Sharing in the Druze Village," in *The Symbolic Role of Animals in Archaeology* (ed. K. Ryan and P. J. Crabtree; Masca Research Papers in Science and Archaeology; Philadelphia: MASCA/University of Pennsylvania Museum of Archaeology and Anthropology, 1995), 74.

[16] Under certain circumstances, multigrain bread was baked. The prophet Ezekiel was instructed to "take wheat, barley, broad beans, lentils, millet, and emmer wheat, and mixing them all in one bowl make your bread from them" (Ezek 4:9). This was not a daily occurrence and came to symbolize poverty and harsh conditions.

[17] The term *ʿuggat raṣāpîm* (1 Kgs 19:6) might refer to bread made on hot coals (Stephen A. Reed, "Bread," *ABD* 1:777–80).

[18] The same scene depicted in Judg 5:25 suggests the possibility that Jael offered Sisera processed milk in a form similar to *ayran,* a Turkish drink made of yogurt thinned with water.

[19] *ANET,* 20.

[20] Borowski, *Every Living Thing,* 140–44.

[21] The bedouin still continue to prepare meat on festive occasions in this manner. The Druze boil the meat in water or *lebani* (thin yogurt) (Grantham, "Dinner in Buqata," 76).

[22] Ibid.; Joel D. Klenck, "Bedouin Animal Sacrifice Practices: Case Study in Israel," in *The Symbolic Role of Animals in Archaeology* (ed. K. Ryan and P. J. Crabtree; Masca Research Papers in Science and Archaeology; Philadelphia: MASCA/University of Pennsylvania Museum of Archaeology and Anthropology, 1995), 57–72.

[23] Klenck, "Bedouin Animal Sacrifice Practices," 71.

[24] The *ashar* gets certain parts of the animal in return for the service he renders, similarly to the contributions given to the priests (Deut 18:3).

[25] Borowski, *Every Living Thing,* 215.

[26] Grantham, "Dinner in Buqata," 73.

[27] The Egyptians knew how to salt not just fish but also fowl. Wen-Amon reports of a shipment of thirty baskets of fish that he received from Egypt (*ANET,* 28).

[28] Brothwell and Brothwell, *Food in Antiquity,* 54 and fig. 18.

[29] During the Roman-Byzantine period, the citron became prominent in Jewish mosaics.

[30] Sesame is used as food in various ways. The seeds are eaten dry and can be added to several dishes as condiment; the leftovers after expressing the oil are eaten as a cake. It can be ground and made into paste that, with the addition of water, is made into a sauce known in Arabic as *tehina.*

[31] One *ʾēpâ* = 5.8 U.S. gallons.

[32] Other plants used for spicing were onion, garlic, and possibly fenugreek.

[33] Klaas A. D. Smelik, *Writings from Ancient Israel: A Handbook of Historical and Religious Documents* (Louisville: Westminster John Knox, 1991), 106. See, e.g., the story of the Gibeonites (Josh 9:3–17).

[34] Borowski, *Every Living Thing,* 56.

[35] Here I do not include installations such as wine and olive presses or threshing floors.

[36] The term Tower of Ovens (Neh 3:11) suggests the existence of public ovens. Bakers' Street (Jer 37:21) suggests the existence of professional bakers who baked for urbanites who could not or did not want to bake.

[37] Whoever suffers of it is *'iwwēr* (Lev 19:14).

[38] Whoever suffers of it is *pissēaḥ* (Lev 21:18).

[39] This story is quite similar to the one told about Elisha (2 Kgs 4:18–37). Was this an early form of mouth-to-mouth resuscitation?

[40] For a complete discussion of this procedure, see Joe Zias, *Cranial Surgery in the Near East: The Anthropological Evidence* (unpublished, n.d.).

[41] For a detailed discussion of hygiene in biblical times, see Edward Neufeld, "Hygiene Conditions in Ancient Israel (Iron Age)," *BA* 34 (1971): 42–66.

[42] Neufeld, "Hygiene Conditions," 58.

[43] Neufeld, "Hygiene Conditions," 63–64.

[44] Jane M. Cahill, Karl Reinhard, David Tarler, and Peter Warnock, "It Had to Happen: Scientists Examine Remains of Ancient Bathroom," *BAR* 17/3 (1991): 63–69; Karl Reinhard and Peter Warnock, "Archaeoparasitology and the Analysis of the Latrine Pit Soils from the City of David," in *Illness and Healing in Ancient Times* (ed. M. Rosovsky; Haifa: Hecht Museum, 1996), 20–23.

[45] Cahill, Reinhard, Tarler, and Warnock, "It Had to Happen," 69.

[46] Without appearing too simplistic, I interpret Israelite society and its culture against its rural background and the economic needs that it generated.

[47] For more on sex in Israelite society, see Lyn M. Bechtel, "Sex," *EDB*, 1192–93; and Tikvah S. Frymer-Kensky, "Sex and Sexuality," *ABD* 5:1144–46.

[48] Although its date of composition is not clear, the Song of Songs reflects this attitude.

[49] For more on prostitution in Old Testament times, see Elaine Adler Goodfriend, "Prostitution: Old Testament," *ABD* 5:505–10; and Kathleen A. Farmer, "Harlot," *EDB*, 552–53. Cult prostitution was forbidden in biblical circles, but we cannot know how much of it was practiced.

[50] The city of Tirzah, one of the capital cities of the northern kingdom, was located in the territory of Manasseh and might have had a relationship to the original holdings of the Zelophehad family.

[51] For more on marriage, see Jon L. Berquist, "Marriage," *EDB*, 861–62; and Christopher J. H. Wright, "Family," *ABD* 2:761–68.

[52] Esau was forty years old (Gen 26:34) and Joseph about thirty years old (Gen 41:46) when they first got married. While this does not appear to be the rule, it seems to be too old when compared with life expectancy.

[53] The story about Samson trying to marry a Philistine woman (Judg 14:10–18) depicts a seven-day feast, but it was only for the young men (a forerunner of the bachelor's party?).

[54] For more on death and burial, see Elizabeth Bloch-Smith, "Burials: Israelite," *ABD* 1:785–89; Elizabeth Bloch-Smith, *Judahite Burial Practices and Beliefs about the Dead* (JSOTSup 123; Sheffield: JSOT Press, 1992); R. Dennis Cole, "Burial," *EDB*, 203–5; Charles A. Kennedy, "Dead, Cult of The," *ABD* 2:105–8; Theodore J. Lewis, "Dead, Abode of The," *ABD* 3:101–5; Kent Harold Richards, "Death: Old Testament," *ABD* 2:108–10.

[55] Other terms for this entity are *šaḥat* and *bôr*.

[56] A similar custom is still practiced in modern rural China.

CHAPTER 5

[1] See, e.g., the clay plaque from Late Bronze Dan known as "The Dancer from Dan," which shows a male dancer playing a lute (Biran, *Biblical Dan*, fig. 84).

[2] His brother Jabal was "the ancestor of all tent-dwellers who raise flocks and herds," and his half-brother Tubal-cain was "the master of all coppersmiths and blacksmiths" (Gen 4:20, 22). Some scholars suggest that *'ûgāb* is a wind instrument (see below), but it is extremely difficult to identify biblical terms with the proper musical instruments they represent.

[3] *ANET,* 288.

[4] For more details, see Joachim Braun, *Music in Ancient Israel/Palestine: Archaeological, Written, and Comparative Sources* (trans. D. W. Stott; Grand Rapids: Eerdmans, 2002); Joachim Braun, "Music, Musical Instruments," *EDB,* 927–30; Ivor H. Jones, "Musical Instruments," *ABD* 4:934–39; Ann Draffkorn Kilmer and Daniel A. Foxvog, "Music," *HBD,* 714–20; Bo Lawergren, "Distinctions among Canaanite, Philistine, and Israelite Lyres, and Their Global Lyrical Contexts," *BASOR* 309 (1998): 41–68; Victor H. Matthews, "Music in the Bible," *ABD* 4:930–34.

[5] The term translated here as "zither" (in Aramaic also *kithara*) is probably the "concert kithara," the most prestigious instrument in Greece (ca. 625–375 B.C.E.). For remarks concerning this instrument, see Lawergren, "Distinctions."

[6] Dothan, *The Philistines,* 250 pl. 33.

[7] As suggested above (n. 2), the *ʿûgāb* might have been also a wind instrument, possibly a flute.

[8] The trumpets were played in recent times, and the lowest notes they produced were D and C respectively (British Museum, *Treasures of Tutankamun* [Westerham, Kent: Trustees of the British Museum; Rainbird; Thames & Hudson, 1972], no. 45).

[9] Kilmer and Foxvog, "Music," 715.

[10] Ibid., 717.

[11] Dothan, *The Philistines,* pl. 33; Dothan and Dothan, *People of the Sea,* pl. 7.

[12] Some scholars translate *ʿûgāb* as lute; others translate *nēbel* as lute.

[13] Lawergren, "Distinctions."

[14] Dothan, *The Philistines,* 233 fig. 8.

[15] Lawergren, "Distinctions." For an example of the number of strings (ten), see Ps 33:2.

[16] Dothan, *The Philistines,* 250 pl. 35.

[17] Kilmer and Foxvog, "Music," 718.

[18] Michalowski, *Art of Ancient Egypt,* pl. 94.

[19] Ibid., pl. 99.

[20] *ANET,* 288.

[21] There is no information about Dan and Bethel during the divided monarchy, but we can assume that things were similar there.

[22] To understand Israelite art in its greater context, see Henri Frankfort, *The Art and Architecture of the Ancient Orient* (4th ed.; New Haven: Yale University Press, 1970); Ann C. Gunter, "Ancient Near Eastern Art," *ABD* 1:402–8.

[23] Tribute and booty lists recorded by the Assyrian kings show that among the trophies they received from Israelite kings were objects made of gold, ivory, different types of wood, and the like.

[24] For more on the subject of seals, seal impressions, and bullae, see Nahman Avigad, *Bullae and Seals from a Post-Exilic Judean Archive* (Qedem 4; Jerusalem: Institute of Archaeology, Hebrew University of Jerusalem, 1976); Nahman Avigad, *Hebrew Bullae from the Time of Jeremiah: Remnants of a Burnt Archive* (Jerusalem: Israel Exploration Society, 1986); Nahman Avigad and Benjamin Sass, *Corpus of West Semitic Stamp Seals* (Jerusalem: Israel Academy of Sciences and Humanities; Israel Exploration Society; Institute of Archaeology, Hebrew University of Jerusalem, 1997).

[25] Zeev Meshel, *Kuntillet ʿAjrud: A Religious Centre from the Time of the Judaean Monarchy on the Border of Sinai* (Jerusalem: Israel Museum, 1978).

CHAPTER 6

[1] The abecedary from Kuntillet ʿAjrûd indicates that later in the Iron Age II (eighth century B.C.E.) individuals continued to learn to write. This is reinforced by many inscriptions on clay vessels made before and after firing by individuals who did not belong to the intelligentsia.

[2] For more on the inscriptions mentioned here, see P. Kyle McCarter Jr., *Ancient Inscriptions: Voices from the Biblical World* (Washington, D.C.: Biblical Archaeology Society, 1996); Smelik, *Writings from Ancient Israel*.

[3] Both sites yielded several other inscriptions.

[4] On seals and seal impressions, see Avigad, *Bullae and Seals;* Avigad, *Hebrew Bullae from the Time of Jeremiah;* Avigad and Sass, *Corpus of West Semitic Stamp Seals*.

[5] Some scholars doubt the authenticity of these seals.

[6] Smelik, *Writings from Ancient Israel*, 105.

[7] Ibid., 113.

[8] *ANET,* 321.

[9] See Andrew G. Vaughn, *Theology, History, and Archaeology in the Chronicler's Account of Hezekiah* (SBLABS 4; Atlanta: Scholars Press, 1999), 152–57.

[10] Borowski, "Hezekiah's Reforms and the Revolt against Assyria."

[11] For details, see Vaughn, *Theology, History, and Archaeology*, 81–135. Vaughn suggests that "the stamping of the royal jars in Hezekiah's kingdom could have been part of a general program of economic buildup that was broader than mere preparation in the final days or weeks before a particular siege" (141). This can be well related to the economic reforms reflected in the changes made in the Judean weight stones, as hinted above in ch. 3.

CHAPTER 7

[1] The exact dates for King Hezekiah are uncertain, and several scholarly sources list them as 715–687, 721–694, or 727–698 B.C.E. The dates for Sennacherib are well established (704–681 B.C.E.).

INDEX OF BIBLICAL REFERENCES

GENESIS

3:7	31
3:16	81
3:19	31, 83
4:20	135
4:21	87
4:22	34, 135
9:1	81
9:7	81
12:2	81
15:18	81
18:2–8	23
18:4	78
18:6–8	65
18:7	67
18:8	66, 68
18:17–33	57
19:1–11	23
19:2	78
21:3	81
21:4	81
21:10	81
23	57
24	82
24:32	78
24:53	82
25:5–6	81
25:7–9	83
25:26	81
25:29	66
25:34	66
26:3–4	81
26:34	82, 135
27	81
27:3–4	67
27:9	67
28:1–9	82
29	22
29:24	82
29:29	82
30:1	81
30:6	81
30:8	81

30:11	81
30:13	81
30:18	81
30:20	81
30:21	81
30:24	81
31:14–16	82
34	82
34:12	82
35:8	83
35:19–20	83
36:2	82
37:25	58
38	82
38:18	96
41:45	82
41:46	135
43:24	78
46:30	83
48:13–20	81
49:13	58

EXODUS

2:16–19	22
3:8	29, 63
4:11	75
4:25	77, 81
9:9–10	76
14:13–14	36
14:20–21	41
15:1–18	91
15:3	36
15:20–21	91
19:10	79
19:14	79
22:15–16 (Eng. 16–17)	82
22:25-26 (Eng. 26–27)	101
23:19	64
25:5	33
26:14	33
30:18–19	78
30:21	78
32:19	92

34:26	64
35:7	33
35:23	33
36:14	35
36:19	35
39:3	32
39:34	35
40:30–31	78

LEVITICUS

1:14	64
2:13	72
5:7	64
6:13–14 (Eng. 20–21)	71
6:20	79
7:9	66
7:9–10	71
7:12	71
11:9–10	69
11:12	69
11:20–23	64, 72
11:25	79
11:28	79
11:29–30	64
11:40	79
11:41–44	64
13	76
13:6	79
13:34	79
13:47–48	32
13:54–55	79
13:58	79
14:8–9	79
15	79
19:14	75, 135
21:17–18	75
21:18	75, 135
21:20	75
22:19–25	75
25:8–55	26
26:25	77
26:26	66, 73

NUMBERS

6:24–26	100
11:5	29
12	76
13	38
14:37	77
17:13–15	77
20:1	83
21:14	106
21:16–18	90
21:27–30	91
21:32	38
25:8–18	77
26:33	82
27:1–11	82
33:39	83
36:2–12	82

DEUTERONOMY

7:15	75
8:7–10	28
8:8	6, 71
8:9	6
8:10	63
10:6	83
12:10	29
14:5	67
14:6	64
14:9	64
14:9–10	69
14:12–18	64
14:21	64
15:2–15	76
18:3	134
18:11	83
20:5–7	37
20:8	37
21:1–9	21
21:6	78
21:15–17	81
21:18	21
21:18–19	16
21:19	21
21:22–23	83
22:6	69
22:8	19
22:13–21	82
22:15	16, 21
22:22–26	82
22:24	16
22:28–29	82
23:2–9 (Eng. 23:1–8)	22

23:13–14 (Eng. 12–13)	80
24:1–4	82
24:12–13	101
25:5–10	82
27:15	34
28:22	76
28:27	75, 76
28:28	75
28:61	75
32:13–18	74
34:6	83

JOSHUA

2	38
2:1–8	23
2:24	39
5:2–3	81
5:3–4	77
6:3–16	91
6:16	39
7:2–3	38
8	40
8:10	21
8:28	41
8:29	41
9:1	4
9:3–17	134
9:3–27	37
9:14–15	39
10	37
10:8–14	36
10:11–13	37
10:13	106
10:26–27	41, 83
10:31–39	36
11:1–9	36
11:2	2
11:3	7
11:11	41
11:12–14	36
11:13	41
11:16	2
11:21	2
12:1	2
12:8	2
13:5	2
15:32	15
17:3–6	82
17:11	14
17:15	2
19:26	2
24:12	37

24:30	83
24:32	83
24:33	83

JUDGES

1:7	41
1:8	41
1:22–24	38
1:22–26	40
3:11	35
3:16	36
3:17	133
3:27	38, 91
3:31	36
4:1–2	37
4:5	22
4:11	34
4:17–22	23
4:19	66, 70
5	36, 40, 41, 91
5:4–5	37
5:14	99
5:17	58
5:20–21	37
5:24	34
5:24–27	23
5:25	70, 134
5:30	32
5:31	36
6:11–21	23
6:18–19	67
6:19	23
6:19–20	67
6:24–32	24
6:34	38, 91
7:3	37
7:5	38
7:9–14	38
7:15	39
7:15–21	91
7:16–22	40
7:25	41
8:16	41
8:17	40
8:21	41
8:32	83
9:34	40
9:34–55	36
9:40	40
9:43–44	40
9:45	41
9:46–52	40

9:46–53	40	10:10–13	24	4:4	75
11:34	41, 91	11:7	38	5:6–8	75
11:40	92	11:15–18	47	5:6–9	60
14	83	11:23–24	47	5:11	33
14:10–18	135	13:3	38	6:5	92
14:15	36	13:8–10	39	6:14–15	92
16:2–3	40	13:19–22	34, 36	8:4	59
16:31	83	14:1–16	40	8:15–18	53
17–18	22, 24	14:36	40	8:17	99
19	23	15:33	41	8:18	59
19:15	21	16:14–23	75	9	24
19:16–27	21	16:16–23	91	9:13	75
19:21	21, 78	17	36, 40	10:3	59
19:22	21	17:17–18	36	10:18	59
19:27	21	17:38	36	11	59
19:29	38	17:45	36	11–12	60
20:1	127	17:51	36, 41	11:2	78
20:16	36	17:54	41	12:31	60
20:27	38	18:6–7	91	13:23–28	25
20:29–41	40	18:13	36	13:37–38	60
21	23	18:25	82	14:28	90
21:19–21	91	18:25–27	41	15:10	92
21:19–23	82	20	25	19:25	78
		20:18–42	38	19:27	75
RUTH		20:19	36	19:36 (Eng 35)	92
2	22	21:14 (Eng 13)	75	20:14–15	60
2:9	65	22:7	36	20:23	59
2:14	65	23:7	40	20:23–26	53
3:3	78	25 23,	25	20:24	102
4	21	25:41	78	22	91
4:1	21	26:5	38	22:21	78
4:1–11	16	26:5–12	40	22:43	79
4:2	21	27:7–12	40	23:8–39	59
		28	83	24:13–17	77
1 SAMUEL		28:3	83		
1	24	28:6	39	**1 KINGS**	
1:3	67, 93	28:24	67	1:34	92
1:21	93	30:1–3	40	1:39	92
2:1–10	91	30:7–8	39	1:40	92
4	37, 39	30:26	36	1:41	92
4:3	21	31:9	41	3:1	60
5:6–12	76	31:12	83	4	53
7:15–17	22	31:12–13	83	4:6	102
8:11–13	22			5:2–3 (Eng. 4:22–23)	65
8:20	59	**2 SAMUEL**		5:3 (Eng. 4:23)	69
9:1	22	1:17–27	41, 91	5:4–5 (Eng. 4:24–25)	60
9:22–24	68	1:18	106	5:6 (Eng. 4:26)	60
9:23–24	67	2:13–17	59	5:18 (Eng. 5:4)	35
9:25	19	2:14–15	40	5:20 (Eng. 5:6)	33
10:2	83	2:32	83	5:22 (Eng. 5:8)	6
10:5	91, 92	3:12–21	59	5:24 (Eng. 5:10)	6
10:5–6	24	3:32–34	92	5:28 (Eng. 5:14)	102

5:32 (Eng. 5:18)	33	9:1–12	75	11:10–47	59
6:29	51	9:20	75	12:1–22	59
6:32	51	10:34	105	12:23–38	59
6:35	51	11:14	92	14:1	33
7	35	12:12	33	15:16–24	92
7:14	35	12:20	105	17	77
7:36	51	13:8	105	18:4	59
8:37	75	13:14	77	18:15–17	53
8:63–66	65	14:15	105	20:3	60
9:15	60	14:18	105	20:4–8	59
9:16	82	14:28	105	21:15	77
9:19	51, 60	15:5	76	21:27	77
9:26–28	58	15:6	105	25:1	92
10:11–12	56, 58	15:11	105	25:1–7	87
10:18	93	15:15	105	27:25–31	53
10:28–29	56	15:16–22	60	27:32–34	53
14:29	105	15:21	105		
15:7	105	15:26	105	**2 Chronicles**	
15:23	105	15:29	61	1:16–17	56, 58
15:31	105	15:31	105	3:5	51
16:14	105	15:36	105	4:6	78
16:27	105	16:19	105	5:12	88
17:8–16	24	17:1–20	61	5:12–13	91
17:17–24	77	17:5	61	7:5–9	65
17:19	18	18:9–17	61	8:6	51, 60
17:23	18	18:17	78	8:9	60
18:26–28	92	18:26	8	8:17–18	56, 58
19:6	134	19:35	77	9:1–13	56
22:4	60	20:7	76	9:17	93
22:5–28	39	20:20	105	9:25	60
22:26	102	21:13	74	9:28	60
22:34	60	21:17	105	12:9	60
22:34–35	60	21:25	105	13:23 (Eng. 14:1)	35
22:39	93, 105	22:6	33	14:4–6 (Eng. 14:5–7)	35
22:46	105	22:14	53	14:7–14 (Eng. 14:8–15)	60
22:49	58	23:8	48, 102, 127	16:1–6	60
22:50	58	23:11	96	17:2	60
		23:28	105	17:12–19	60
2 Kings		24:1–2	61	18:33	60
1:2	77, 130	24:5	105	18:33–34	60
1:18	105	24:10–17	61	19:3	59
3:4	32	24:14	35	20:35–37	59
3:15	92	24:14–16	61	21:18–19	77, 80
4:8–11	24	25:1–4	61	24:12	33
4:10	18, 20	25:1–21	61	24:23	60
4:18–37	135	25:19–21	61	24:25	77
4:39–40	64			25:5–10	60
5	76, 78	**1 Chronicles**		25:11–14a	60
8:1–6	26	4:23	31	25:17–24	60
8:20–21	60	6:31	92	26:6–8	60
8:21	60	7:15	82	26:9–10	60
8:23	105	11:4–8	60	26:11–15	60

26:19	76	24:8	36	36:11	8
27:3–4	60	33:2	136	38:2–7	76
27:5	60	41:4	75	38:10	83
28:5–6	60	45:9	94	40:19	35
28:7–15	61	60:10	78	41:7	35
28:16–21	61	68	92	41:25	31
28:17–19	60	72	92	42:13	36
30	24	89	92	44:12	34, 35
30:23–24	133	101	92	44:13	33
32	61	108:10	78	44:16	67
33:10–13	61	110	92	44:19	66, 67
33:14	60, 69	120–134	93	45:9	31
35:15	88, 93	128:3	81	46:6	35
35:20–24	60	144	92	48:10	35
36:6–7	61			50:1	82
36:10	61	**PROVERBS**		54:16	35
36:17–20	61	3:8	75	57:20	79
36:20	61	16:24	71	64:8	31
		31:13	32		
EZRA		31:15	26, 74	**JEREMIAH**	
2:41	93	31:19	32	2:22	63, 78
2:65	93	31:24	57	3:8	82
3:10	93			5:27–28	54
		ECCLESIASTES		6:1	103
NEHEMIAH		3:1–8	ix	6:29	35
3:3	69			7:17–18	54
3:11	134	**SONG OF SONGS**	135	16:5	84
3:13	55	5:3	78	18:3	31
12:38	55	7:1 (Eng. 6:13)	91	19:10–11	31
12:39	69			22:3	54
		ISAIAH		22:13–17	54
ESTHER		1:25	35	24:1	33, 35
6:1	104	5:8	54	25:30	90
		5:26–28	37	29:2	33, 35
JOB		7:3	55, 78	30:6	76
2:7	76	7:15	133	30:13	75
2:8	31	7:22	133	32:6–15	101
6:6	72	10:14	69	32:6–44	26
9:30	78	11–12	54	32:10–14	96
15:27	133	13	37	32:44	96
21:11–12	90	13:8	75	33:6	75
22:30	78	14:15	83	34:7	103
42:15	82	17:11	75	36:10	100
		19:9	32	36:18	100
PSALMS		21	54	36:32	100
2	92	21:3	75	37:21	55, 134
12:7	35	22:15–16	100	46:1–10	37
18:21	78	23:8	57	46:11	75
18:25	78	29:16	31	48:32–33	90
18:43	79	30:14	31		
19:11	71	33:9	2	**LAMENTATIONS**	
20	92	36:2	55, 78	4:2	31

EZEKIEL
4:9 134
4:12 80
16:3 128
16:45 128
17:4 57
17:10 6
27–28 58
28:4–5 57
30:21 75
31:15 83
34:3 32

DANIEL
3:5 88
3:7 88
3:10 88
3:15 88

HOSEA
12:8 57

13:2 35

AMOS
2:6–8 54
3:15 94
4:1 54, 133
5:7–12 54
5:12 16
5:15 16
5:23 92
6:1–7 54
6:4–5 91
6:4–6 74
6:7 84
8:5–6 54

JONAH 133

MICAH
7:10 79

ZEPHANIAH
1:10 69
1:11 57

ZECHARIAH
9:3 79
10:5 79
12:4 75
14:21 57

MALACHI
3:2 78
3:2–3 35
3:20 75

INDEX OF MODERN AUTHORITIES

Aharoni, Yohanan 10, 127
Avi-Yonah, Michael 10, 127
Avigad, Nahman 107, 136, 137
Avitsur, Shmuel 85, 131, 134
Ayalon, Etan 85, 131, 134
Bechtel, Lyn M. 135
Benjamin, Don C. 41, 130, 132
Berquist, Jon L. 135
Biblical Archaeologist 52
Biran, Avraham 61, 131, 132, 133, 135
Blenkinsopp, Joseph 130, 131
Bloch-Smith, Elizabeth 85, 135
Borowski, Oded 41, 127, 129, 130, 131, 132, 133, 134, 137
Braun, Joachim 98, 136
Briquel-Chatonnet, Françoise 127
British Museum 8
Broshi, Magen 128
Brothwell, Don R. 85, 133, 134
Brothwell, Patricia 85, 133, 134
Cahill, Jane M. 135
Cole, R. Dennis 135
Dar, Shimon 129, 130
Dever, William G. 10, 128, 132, 133
Dothan, Moshe 127, 136
Dothan, Trude 127, 136
Lipiński, Edward 127
Farmer, Kathleen A. 135
Finkelstein, Israel 10, 128, 129, 133
Foxvog, Daniel A. 136
Frankel, Rafael 85, 131, 134
Frankfort, Henri 98, 136
Friend, Glenda 131
Fritz, Volkmar 129, 130, 131
Frymer-Kensky, Tikva 135
Goodfriend, Elaine Adler 135
Gophna, Ram 129
Grantham, Bill 134
Gubel, Eric 127
Gunter, Ann C. 98, 136
Hallo, William W. 11
Hardin, James W. 130
Herzog, Ze'ev 15, 16, 17, 43, 45, 48, 61,
128, 129, 131, 132
Hesse, Brian 133
Israel Antiquities Authority 88, 89, 94
Israel Exploration Society 19, 50
Israel Museum, Jerusalem 25
Jones, Ivor H. 136
Karges, Dylan 110
Kennedy, Charles A. 135
Kilmer, Ann Draffkorn 136
King, Philip J. 127
Klenck, Joel D. 134
Lawergren, Bo 136
Lewis, Theodore J. 135
Liver, Jacob 131
Malamat, Abraham 131
Matthews, Victor H. 41, 130, 132, 136
Mazar, Amihai 1, 11, 127, 129, 131
McCarter, P. Kyle, Jr. 107, 137
Meshel, Zeev 95, 136
Meyers, Carol 41, 129, 130
Michalowski, Kazimierz 133, 136
Netzer, Ehud 18, 42, 130
Neufeld, Edward 85, 135
Paul, Shalom M. 132
Pritchard, James B. 11, 128, 131, 133, 134, 136, 137
Rad, Gerhard von 131
Reed, Stephen A. 134
Reich, Ronny 61, 132
Reinhard, K. 135
Reviv, Hanoch 130, 132
Richards, Kent Harold 135
Ronen, Yigal 133
Sass, Benjamin 107, 136, 137
Schloen, J. David 42, 130
Shanks, Hershel 132
Shiloh, Yigal 62, 128, 129, 130, 131, 132
Shukron, Eli 132
Singer-Avitz, Lily 130
Smelik, Klaas A. D. 102, 107, 134, 137
Stager, Lawrence E. 42, 127, 129
Stern, Ephraim 127
Tarler, David 135

Ussishkin, David	9, 62, 128, 132	Wright, George R. H.	62, 131, 132
Vanderkam, James C.	131	Yadin, Yigael	103, 131, 133
Vaughn, Andrew G.	x, 101, 102, 103,	Yassin, K.	129
107, 137		Younger, K. Lawson, Jr.	11
Walsh, Carey Ellen	131	Yurco, Frank J.	7, 128
Wapnish, Paula	133	Zertal, Adam	127, 129, 131
Warnock, Peter	135	Zevit, Ziony	42, 130, 132
Wood, Bryant G.	131	Zias, Joe	135
Wright, Christopher J. H.	135		

INDEX OF HEBREW WORDS

ʾăbaʿbūʿōt	76	ṭabbāḥ	67
ʾaḥuzzâ	26	ṭabbūn	66
ʾillēm	75	ṭəḥōrîm	76
ʾāsîp	28	ṭîṭ ḥûṣôt	79
ʾēpâ	71, 134	yəhûdît	8
ʾărûkâ	75	yḥwḥ	106
ʾarmôn	50	yôbēl	89
ʾăšer ʿal habbayit	53, 100	yôṣēr	31
bāmâ	55	yôreh	6
ben hammelek	102	yērāqôn	76
bənôtêhā	14	yātēd	80
beqaʿ, bqʿ	57, 106	kəʾēb	75
bôr	135	kbs	78
barbūrîm ʾăbûsîm	69	khnm	106
brr	78	kinnôr	87, 89, 91, 92
bōrît	78	kor	65, 133
bêt ʾāb	16, 20, 21, 22	kittim	103
bat hammelek	102	lbyt	106
bêt haššēn	94	leḥem	66
bêt melek	50	lmlk	96, 104
gērû	57	ləraggēl	38
deber	77	lattûr	38
dəbaš	29, 70	maggēpâ	75, 77
dāgâ	69	madweh	75
dəway	75	māzôr	75
dalleqet	76	mizmôr	90
hêkāl	50	malʾāk	77
har	2	malqôš	6
har ʾeprāyim	2	mûm	75
har yəhûdâ	2	mmšt	96, 104
har yiśrāʾēl	2	mənaʿănʿîm	88
haśśār	101	mənaṣṣēaḥ	90
ziqnê hāʿîr	21	miskənôt	51
ḥebel	75	məṣiltayim	88
ḥŏlî	75	maṣṣēbôt	55
ḥālîl	89, 91, 92	maṣṣôt	28
ḥōmeṣ	134	məraggəlîm	38
ḥăṣōṣərâ	89	marzēaḥ	84
ḥăṣērîm	15	marḥešet	74
ḥereb	76, 77	marpēʾ	75
ḥarḥur	76	maśkîl	90
ḥēreš	75	mišpāḥâ	21, 22
ḥāraš ʿēṣîm	33	mašrôqîtāʾ	88

maštîn baqqîr	80	*qaddaḥat*	76
nēbel	89, 91, 92, 136	*qdš*	106
negaʿ	75	*qeren*	89
nəḥîlôt	89	*qarnāʾ*	88
naḥălâ	26, 82, 83	*qaṭros*	88
naʿar	102	*rûaḥ ḥaqqādîm*	6
neṣep, nṣp	57, 106	*rəḥôb*	21
neter	78	*rāʿāb*	77
sabkāʾ	88	*rəpūʾôt*	75
sûmpônyâ	88	*ripʾût*	75
sôpēr	99	*rəpāʾîm*	83
sôpərîm	99	*repeš ḥûṣôt*	79
sîr	78	*śar ʾelep*	36
sōləlâ	60	*śar ḥāʿîr*	53, 102
sēper kərîtût	82	*šəʾôl*	83
ʿebed	53, 102	*šābūʿôt*	28
ʿuggat rəṣāpîm	134	*šiggāʿôn*	75
ʿûgāb	87, 135, 136	*šiddāpôn*	76
ʿiwwēr	135	*šôpēṭ*	21
ʿiwwārôn	75	*šôpəṭîm*	21, 36
ʿăliyyâ	18	*šôpār*	38, 89, 91, 92
ʿōpel	48	*šəḥîn*	76
pym	57, 106	*šaḥepet*	76
pəsantərîn	88	*šaḥat*	135
pissēaḥ	135	*šîr*	90
paʿămôn	88	*šēkār*	71
ṣēʾātekā	80	*šālîš*	88
ṣûp	71	*šillūḥîm*	82
ṣîr	75	*təhillâ*	90
ṣelṣelîm	88	*tōp, tôp*	89, 91, 92
ṣinnôr	60, 133	*təpillâ*	90
ṣārāʿat	76		